Using Stories to Build Bridges with Traumatized Children

USING STORIES TO BUILD BRIDGES WITH TRAUMATIZED CHILDREN

Creative Ideas for Therapy, Life Story Work, Direct Work and Parenting

Kim S. Golding

Forewords by Steve Killick amd Dan Hughes

Illustrated by Julia McConville

Jessica Kingsley *Publishers*
London and Philadelphia

First published in 2014
by Jessica Kingsley Publishers
73 Collier Street
London N1 9BE, UK
and
400 Market Street, Suite 400
Philadelphia, PA 19106, USA

www.jkp.com

Library of Congress Cataloging in Publication Data
Golding, Kim S., author.
  Using stories to build bridges with traumatized children : creative ideas for therapy, life
story work,
direct work and parenting / Kim S. Golding ; foreword by Steve Killick ; illustrations by
Julia McConville.
    pages cm
  Includes bibliographical references and index.
  ISBN 978-1-84905-540-6
1. Psychic trauma in children--Treatment. 2. Post-traumatic stress disorder in children--
Treatment.
3. Storytelling. 4. Narrative therapy. I. Title.
  RJ506.P66G65 2014
  618.92'8521--dc23
                                2014001086

British Library Cataloguing in Publication Data
A CIP catalogue record for this book is available from the British Library

ISBN 978 1 84905 540 6
eISBN 978 0 85700 961 6

Printed and bound in Great Britain

I would like to dedicate this book to the memory of my grandmother, Deborah Golding, and my father, Charles Peter Golding, whose delight in story creation has stayed with me throughout my life.

Contents

Part IV: Keep Noticing Me

Part V: Learning about Relationships

Part VI: Stories for Parents

Part VII: Stories for Practitioners

Appendices

List of Stories

Foreword

We are lonesome animals. We spend all our life trying to be less lonesome. One of our ancient methods is to tell a story begging the listener to say – and to feel – 'Yes, that's the way it is, or at least that's the way I feel it. You're not as alone as you thought.'

(Steinbeck 1930)

I first met Kim ten years ago when she was running a training session on Attachment Theory. The workshop, which took place in the drab surrounds of a disused ward in a psychiatric hospital, had a big impact for many of us there about how we thought about Attachment Theory. Looking back, I can really see the influence that that session had on me. One of the things I most clearly remember was Kim's use of scenarios to illustrate how children's attachment patterns influenced their behaviour. This captured my imagination, and I used the stories when I began working with foster carers to help them begin to understand how relationships can determine behaviour. Stories have the potential to demonstrate such situations more clearly than any other form of explanation. Of course I was not the only person to be influenced by Kim. Ten years on, many professionals working with children in the UK, particularly those working in the looked-after system, are using these ideas. Kim's work helped transform the understanding of many people about Attachment Theory. It changed from being a theory we knew but were unsure of its clinical applications to one where we saw its importance in all modes of therapy. Kim has championed these ideas, and her skill and expertise in doing so has influenced so many people in their practice. She has been a leading light in the development of this area and her publications are truly valuable resources, especially for those working with traumatized children. This book is one that can be added to the list of such resources and it is a privilege to be able to introduce this fascinating insight into using stories. Stories and storytelling are, I believe, undervalued tools for helping children and adults learn about their feelings, their inner world of wishes and desires, and for giving them the experience of feeling *understood*.

Many might see storytelling as a pleasant and fun activity but, apart from developing language and literacy skills, not having a great impact on a child's development. This view is changing as more is now understood of the importance of both fictional and non-fictional narratives upon how children think and understand relationships. A key task for children growing and learning how to survive in this world is knowing their own feelings, their fears and desires, and to understand these as part of being human. They have to learn that their experiences of feeling rejected, loved and loving, of feeling competent or incompetent and valued or worthless, are part of the experience of living that are faced by all. Children who experience trauma and abuse often face a much tougher task in learning these lessons than those who do not. We learn about these things through stories, for we are always surrounded by them. A child learns about who they are through the stories the adults in their lives tell about them, they learn about their families and heritage through the family stories they may (or may not) hear. They learn about their culture through the myths, fairy tales and hi(stories) they are exposed to, through computer or television screens, books or told face to face. These stories all contribute to the development of an identity, that in itself is no more than a story, one that can either be helpful and dynamic or restrictive and unhelpful. The stories in this book, created from both the realities of children's lives and a liberating imagination, show how storymaking and storytelling can help children understand themselves better and see themselves differently. It illustrates, as stories clearly can, the almost magical power of storytelling to transform and heal.

All children can benefit and grow through stories. Stories undoubtedly help children learn about their inner world, and it gives a language for their emotions and experiences. Indeed, stories may be so beneficial that, as philosopher Denis Dutton (2010) suggests, they may offer an evolutionary advantage as they provide a way of talking about inner experience and from learning of the experience of others. In stories we find a way of voicing the inner thoughts and feelings, the intentions, the defeats and victories of the characters in the story. Stories are, as Margot Sunderland (2000) has said, the natural way that children learn about their feelings. They don't learn about this half as well through explanation and reasoning. Of course, a foundation comes through the empathic responses of caregivers that helps them to name and learn about their feelings, but particular insights can be given through stories that can name our darkest impulses. We are drawn to stories for this emotional experience, and it can go a long way in transforming impulsive acting-out behaviour to something more reflective – to be able to pause and think about an action. We have various terms that name this ability to think about our emotional experience: mentalization, emotional literacy and reflective thinking amongst others. These terms have much in common with each other; they allude to the ability to recognize thoughts, feelings and motivations in both ourselves and others and to use this information to guide our actions. However it is termed, the foundation is laid in the process of 'intersubjectivity', the process by which people experience themselves through their interactions with others. This is at the very heart of the attachment relationship and, as Kim reveals, storytelling is at the heart of this intersubjective process. The adult carer constructs narratives about the child's experiences, which not only gives a language for thoughts and feelings but influences how they will come to see themselves, hopefully as loveable and competent human beings, able to deal with the problems life may bring.

So stories and storytelling are part of loving relationships and, like those relationships, build a healthy sense of self. For children who have experienced trauma, neglect or other abuse, often in ambivalent or unsafe relationships, the need for healthy relationships is great. Many children in care, lacking the blueprint for dealing with feelings and relationships, often struggle, even when their circumstances may have seemed to improve. Stories have a very important part in helping them make sense of their thoughts and feelings and to find ways of growing and changing.

Another important aspect of stories is that they are rich in symbol, image and metaphor. Metaphor, particularly, is one of the ways we can understand our own inner experience by likening it to processes in the physical world. In stories we learn about how the physical, social and interior worlds work. Consider the wealth of information contained in a traditional story such as 'The Three Little Pigs' – we learn that everybody, even pigs, must leave the protection of their mother and find their home. We learn that houses can be made in different ways, and some are stronger and more secure than others. We learn that the world is full of dangers, of people or creatures that may be threatening to us. Most importantly, we learn that these dangers can be overcome, and safety and happiness can be found. So we can learn, effortlessly and joyfully, about how the world and minds work through stories. Many stories are clearly not true; we learn early that animals don't really talk and that some things are not physically possible – pigs don't build houses, but we can still enjoy and engage with the story. We learn that the truths of stories are not factual but metaphorical and narrative in nature. Stories allow us to test our knowledge of reality – we wonder if the story is true or not.

It is the power of metaphor to transform meanings that is often forgotten. Life story work is, of course, critical for helping children overcome trauma, but it is much more than learning about the 'facts' of one's life. Stories are more than facts; they are also about meaning and relationships. This is not to say that the facts of a child's life are not as important as the 'story' they hold about themselves; such facts are very important to know, but it is the 'story' that gives meaning to them. All of us are telling stories about ourselves to ourselves all the time, and we might understand the concept of 'self' as 'a constantly changing set of stories'. Kim's stories use metaphors simply and artfully. In one story the transition from caterpillar to butterfly becomes analogous to growing up and separating, of taking flight as an autonomous person. It is a metaphor of transformation and can transform how people see themselves. The metaphor of a bridge, from another of the stories and the title of this book, also reflects transition by using an object in the physical world to suggest a psychological change. Stories that do not come from the world of facts and rational explanations can help the mind find new ways of seeing. These stories are not like facts; they are dynamic and often in flux, changing, growing and developing.

We think in stories, we are *homo narrans*. We are storytelling animals. So we want the stories we tell ourselves about ourselves to be helpful rather than self-limiting or even destructive. One belief many people hold these days is 'I'm not a storyteller' or 'I couldn't tell stories', even though the ability to tell stories is given to us all if we trust ourselves, our imagination and our memories. The human mind is well adapted for storytelling. Kim tells us her process of developing the stories and then shows us the stories, allowing us to see how powerful they are. When I first read them, I thought of the many children I've worked with and felt closer to them, that I understood them better and, in turn, have become more curious about their experience. Kim shows us what we can do when we start thinking about the children we work with using imagination and creativity. She finds inspiration for the stories by attending to her intuitive and imaginative responses to them, and lets that provide the inspiration for communicating her feelings and insights. What better way can we communicate that we are keeping someone in mind than by letting them see that we have entered their dreaming world, their inner landscape of hurts, wishes and fears, and sharing our inner imaginative world too? In a therapeutic world increasingly dominated by 'outcomes', it is very good to be reminded of this.

Steve Killick, Clinical Psychologist and Storyteller

Foreword

There is a story behind this short foreword.

As a very experienced psychologist I sat down to read Kim Golding's new book *Using Stories to Build Bridges with Traumatized Children*. I anticipated a light and relaxing time, and that I would be reading a good deal of what I already knew, presented with Kim's excellent writing abilities. I read Kim's modest goals at the start of the book to provide readers with 'some starting points' that would 'stimulate their creativity' and her reminder that 'we are all story creators'. My early expectations were swept away by rising excitement as I read Kim's work.

I discovered so many new things about stories which I might have known, but had not known so deeply. I learned of many, many reasons why stories have been so helpful in our personal and cultural development over thousands of years. I learned of the many types of stories that help us with our developmental stages, to solve problems, resolve traumas, discover new aspects of relationships with others, and truly 'make sense' of the challenges of living. I also learned to see patterns in how stories develop and feel more confident that I will be more creative in developing my own stories having the 'starting points' that Kim has provided.

How do I end this foreword?

By reflecting on how much I also enjoyed reading the 21 stories which Kim has embedded in this book, ranging from stories for young children to tales for adults, but all designed to help us to understand the power of stories and their potential to help traumatized children.

In reading the book I have directly experienced how stories serve as a great way for us to deeply learn important matters while at the same time feeling safe and engaged in the process. Kim Golding is truly both an excellent psychologist, teacher, and writer while at the same time being a wonderful story creator.

This is a work to read deeply and to keep nearby as we use stories to help children, their families, and ourselves to make sense of our lifelong journeys.

Dan Hughes, Clinical Psychologist

ACKNOWLEDGEMENTS

The inspiration to use stories within my clinical practice has come from so many sources that it is hard to write these acknowledgements. Inevitably I will miss out some important people. Some, however, stand out as being a huge influence on me, giving me confidence both as a story creator and teller. Dan Hughes has storytelling at the heart of his work, and his training and writings have always been an inspiration for me. A number of years ago I was privileged to attend a workshop with Mike White; sadly, Mike is no longer with us, but the memory of his stories and his use of stories in clinical work remain with me. One of the highlights of many years of attending the Annual British Psychological Society Conference for clinical psychologists working with children and families is of Steve Killick entertaining us with an evening storytelling session. Amongst many, these three practitioners have been a huge influence on my own confidence to bring stories into my clinical work.

Personal acknowledgements go to a number of people who have helped me in my writing of this book. Thanks especially to Emily Barnbrook, my colleague and friend, who has always been a willing audience for my stories as I have written them, and for reading and commenting on a draft of this book. Thanks to Steve Killick for also reading and commenting on the draft, and for his contribution of the Foreword for this book. I have also tried out some of my stories at various training events that I have delivered, both within the UK and USA; the generous responses of the people attending these events gave me the confidence to write this book.

My heartfelt thanks go to all the children and their parents who have inspired me to write stories.

As ever, I have a very supportive husband, Chris, who never complains when I become immersed in my writing. I am privileged to have two children, Alex and Lily, who I have supported into adulthood. Their love of story has always given me a lot of pleasure. The beginning of putting this book together occurred during a week with my mother, visiting family in Barnsley, Yorkshire. It seemed very fitting that my mother and I shared stories of her growing up whilst this book was coming into being. Thanks to my cousin Christine for her hospitality, and for making this very overdue trip happen.

Finally, thank you Steve Jones, for continuing to believe in what I am doing, and to all his colleagues at Jessica Kingsley Publishers who take such care of my work.

Introduction

Children and adults alike love stories; it is no surprise therefore that stories are a central resource within therapeutic interventions. Such 'helping stories' are created with a purpose that is beyond entertainment. They are designed to also provide advice, guidance, wisdom or healing. The writer Karen Blixen (aka Isak Dinesen) once attributed a friend as saying that 'All sorrows can be borne if you put them into a story or tell a story about them' (cited in Grosz 2013, p.10). Stories can build connections with others, and thus allow support, facilitating recovery from distress and trauma.

For generations children have been entertained by stories. These can be told, read or watched, alone, or with others. Many children escape into stories when the real world is too overwhelming. Stories evoke curiosity in the child and in this way are a means to stimulate the imagination, educate and, as Bettelheim, the child psychologist and psychoanalyst, suggests, 'clarify the emotions'. In order to do this such stories need to 'be attuned to his [sic] anxieties and aspirations; give full recognition to his difficulties, while at the same time suggesting solutions to the problems which perturb him' (Bettelheim 1991, p.5). This is a good definition for the stories at the centre of this book. I have called these 'helping stories', a general term to encompass the range of stories that can be used therapeutically to provide insight, suggest solutions, facilitate healing, process trauma and understand life story experience.

As the examples in this book illustrate, stories are not just for children but they are also for all of us. Storytelling is a tradition that is found in all cultures. Dan Hughes, a clinical psychologist who has developed a way of working with traumatized children and their families which has storytelling at its heart, writes: 'For centuries, interpersonal influences that have evoked change in many cultures, among many communities, involve communication through storytelling' (Hughes 2011, p.46). If stories can lead to cultural change, then how powerful can they be for facilitating family change? Stories are a way of understanding our experience, helping us to organize what we have experienced and predicting what we might experience next (Freeman, Epston and Lobovits 1997). In fact, Parkinson (2009, p.66) suggests that telling stories is a 'human given'; without stories we would not be fully human. Stories offer the listener a different perspective. They therefore lend themselves to empowering and healing. Stories can be used to overcome fears, share sadness, imagine the fulfilment of a dream, revisit the past and find hope for the future (Thomas and Killick 2007).

I have had the habit of writing stories for many years within my clinical work. Inspired by the children and families, I use the writing of the stories to enhance my own understanding. Often these begin with a single image or metaphor that has come to me as I work with the families. In writing the story inspired by this symbol, I find my own insight is enhanced. The stories rely on metaphor, symbol and themes that mirror but are at a distance from the person or persons who inspired the story. Names are changed, and troubles or burdens disguised through the structure and content of the story. This allows me, and others with whom I share the stories, to find a new perspective or enhanced understanding without the pain or distress of direct contact with the issue. Sense of failure, of hopelessness, of not being good enough are all reduced when we visit our difficulties through the eyes of another. The solutions found by these others can then offer some hope to us, or at least help us to better understand the source of our hopelessness because of the impact the story has had.

In this book I share with you my understanding about creating stories. Drawing upon my experience, together with the wisdom of others, I have written about the use of stories within therapeutic interventions. I follow this with a chapter on story creation for those of you who would like more ideas for how to start or build upon your own story-creating experience. This is followed by a range of stories to illustrate the variety of ways stories can be used in therapeutic work. For each story I have written some notes describing my understanding of the experience of the children and families who inspired the stories. Many of these stories are written with foster and adopted children in mind as these are the children I am working with. Many of these story ideas could, however, be adapted for children in different circumstances. At the end of each part I include some additional notes to reflect upon how such stories might be used in practice.

In writing the stories I inevitably draw upon my own culture and life experience. The examples of stories within this book therefore largely reflect the Western world, and the English countryside. I hope these stories will inspire you to write your own stories full of your own culture and life experience.

Sometimes I share the stories I write with the families, and a new story can emerge in the sharing as we reflect on and respond to the narrative.

Some stories I have written directly for children at a particular point in my therapeutic work. I incorporate characters that I anticipate will appeal to the children; in this way they can identify with this character, allowing them to find their own meaning in the story. Sometimes I take a story or image that the child has shared with me and invent my own story around theirs; thus the story becomes a symbol of our collaborative work together. I read the stories to them; sometimes they respond and sometimes not, but the story rests with them. If they choose to talk about the story I am happy to reflect upon it with them; if they prefer to move on, I trust that the story will be there to help them when they need it. Some children have enjoyed illustrating the stories. Others have delighted in small elements within the story, making up their own around these elements. Storytelling becomes a part of what we do, whether in writing, drawing, playing with puppets or chatting together.

Some of the stories have been written especially for parents, written from my privileged position of being witness to the joys and despairs, the challenges and creative solutions that these parents have found within their parenting of traumatized children. In sharing these stories I hope I can give a new perspective on lived experience. We all create stories for ourselves; often these stories become dominated by our own fears, doubts and worries: 'I am failing', 'This will never work', 'He cannot succeed.' When we share stories, our perspectives are multiplied, and hope can arise out of these alternative understandings. The stories offer different insights into the inner world of child and/ or parent, insights that can lead to greater acceptance and empathy for the difficulties and challenges being faced, and increased security for all family members.

In the last part I have included three stories for practitioners, illustrating how understanding can be enhanced by stories for all of us. These stories convey some of my experience from 14 years of working within a specialist, multi-agency service set up to support looked-after and adopted children and their families. I offer this perspective to illustrate how stories can help those giving and receiving services to have a broader understanding of what we can offer insecure children and their families. As I write, such services are seriously under threat because of budget cuts and under-resourcing of health and social care services, and yet, without such services, the families are left to try and traverse the turbulent waters of family life, lived against the backdrop of trauma, without a strong bridge built from specialist knowledge and understanding.

The bridge metaphor is a recurring one within storytelling traditions. Storytelling is seen as a bridge between inner psychological worlds and outer real worlds (Thomas and Killick 2007). Healing can arise when we build a 'bridge of meaning' with children (Freeman *et al.* 1997, p.xv). The bridge can also symbolize the relationship that all people need to flourish in the world, a metaphor that Simon and Garfunkel used so well in their well-known song. I have used this song as my inspiration for the final story. It sums up my experience of therapeutic services for families caring for displaced and traumatized children as, at their heart, services which are building bridges with the families to help them traverse their own troubled waters.

I hope that this book can inspire you to create your own stories for yourself or for the children you are caring for. As you reflect on the inner as well as the outer experience of what you are living or working with on a daily basis, you will find your horizons are broadened and the bridges leading to these horizons will become stronger.

Notes

1. An age range has been given for each story, based on my own use of these stories. This is flexible, however, as children will vary in their maturity and interest in the stories. Adults, too, can find all the stories helpful, whether or not they were originally written for children.

2. I have alternated the use of 'he' and 'she' throughout the book.

3. I have structured the stories under a range of headings, but there are themes that recur amongst these stories. This structuring therefore organizes the stories but is not intended to limit their use or reduce the perspectives they offer.

1

The Power of Stories to Facilitate Healing for Children and Their Families

A few years ago I was working with a little girl who was living in foster care. This was a long-term placement but she was struggling to believe in the permanence on offer. Her experience of neglect, domestic violence and physical abuse within her family of origin, followed by several short-term foster placements, had left her profoundly distrustful of any parent. She anticipated abandonment and perceived anger and rejection in her single foster parent, even when being offered kindness and a sense of belonging. At the time I was learning to use Dyadic Developmental Psychotherapy, or DDP as it is popularly known (Hughes 2011). My developing use of the therapeutic stance of PACE (Playfulness, Acceptance, Curiosity and Empathy) had made a connection with this little girl who was able to enter into some of the playfulness, whilst being able to explore with us her past terrors and current experience. She talked with me and with her foster mother about hiding beneath the bed when family members were attacking each other, and creeping down in the night to try and find some food in the fridge. These three-year-old memories were telling a story which was evoking empathy in us. In addition, this little girl was able to tell her foster mother how much she heard shouting when this gentle and quiet foster mother had to say 'no' to her – a story about her current experience, linked to her past experience, which helped us to understand why she so often got angry with her foster mother.

In one particular session with this little girl and her foster mother I was rather tired following a night of disturbed sleep as I had helped a family member who was ill. I did not want to cancel the appointment and let the girl down; she was too prone to feeling rejected, and so I decided to meet with her for a short, lighter session before going home to catch up on my sleep. Maybe it was the tiredness, maybe the multiple stories I had been receiving from her, maybe a bit of both, but part-way through the session I found myself telling her a story. There was no plan or forethought in my mind, but intuitively I found a story that connected with the stories she had been sharing with us in previous sessions. I can still remember the stillness and absorption of this young child as I made up the story for her. I remember even more clearly the astonishment of both the foster mother and myself when the child told the story back to me the following week. As far as I could remember, for I had not written the story down, her retelling was word perfect! Following this experience I would often incorporate stories into my DDP-informed therapeutic work.

The structured use of stories within DDP makes a lot of sense. After all, storytelling is at the heart of this intersubjective approach. The affective–reflective dialogue which therapists use with children and parents represents the story that emerges as emotion is regulated and experience is explored. The child is not lectured to; solutions to problems are not sought; but the child's experience is made clearer through the construction of narratives about this experience. This is a collaborative process within which the child gains a deep sense of being understood, communicates this to her parents and receives acceptance and empathy for all she has, and is experiencing. The child develops increased security, and possibilities for what can be are opened up in the process.

Storytelling brings the affective (emotional experience of the story) and the reflective (content of the story) together, with the verbal components of the story being enriched by the non-verbal. This close attention to the affective as well as the reflective is similarly fundamental to DDP. Dan Hughes is the originator of DDP, and anyone who has witnessed his training and his therapeutic work will know that storytelling is at the heart of what he does. He writes about storytelling within DDP:

> This nonverbal, attuned dance among those who are communicating is where the affective component of the dialogue lies. It generates safety, deep interest in the story, and a momentum within the dialogue that calls for increased coherence within the story being created. It invites new events into the storytelling process in a way that makes them much less likely to be avoided or defensively engaged. Once this safety and momentum for completion are generated, there is

openness to making sense of the story that is evolving. This process leads naturally into a greater readiness to reflect on the events that have affected a person, to understand their impact and to invite them into the story. (Hughes 2011, p.46)

Steve Killick and Maria Boffey (2012) discuss the 'three Ts model' of storytelling: the Telling, the Tale and the Talk. This resonates with the components that are so essential to DDP. The Telling represents the playful, interactional, verbal and non-verbal process of telling the story. Storytelling and DDP help children and families enter into intersubjective relationships, connections that involve shared affect, attention and complementary intention. Within these relationships narratives can be co-constructed relating to past and current experience; this is the Tale in the three Ts model. The Talk is the expression of curiosity, acceptance and empathy that comes out of the telling of the tale, talk that will be playful and non-judgmental because it stems from shared stories. PACE is part of DDP and storytelling.

Stories are at the heart of therapy. They have an explicit focus in DDP and other forms of therapy for children and families. Narrative therapy, for example, is a therapeutic intervention built around the constructing of stories that works with the client's own narratives (e.g. Freeman *et al.* 1997; Vetere and Dowling 2005; White 2004; White and Epston 1990). This approach focuses on informal stories told within families. The stories provide an account of family members' experience that is shaping their lives and relationships. This is less about storytelling through metaphor and symbol, but it is about working with the problem-saturated stories held within the families. These are the stories that families contruct which demonstrate their view of a sitaution as a problem. By retelling the story with the family, their perspective can be changed to something more positive. New meanings emerge by viewing the situation differently. The dominant story is reconstructed, allowing alternate stories to emerge.

An alternative approach to working with stories is to facilitate the telling of stories by children (e.g. Salans 2009; Sunderland 2000). Using drama, writing and drawing, children are helped to find stories that help them to 'express muddled and confused experience and feelings. Stories can help a child find the way again' (Jennings 2004, p.29).

Practitioners or parents can create 'helping stories' for children. For example, Lacher, Nichols and May (2005) advise parents to create stories for children with attachment difficulties. They suggest four categories of stories that are helpful for these children: Claiming; Developmental; Trauma; and Successful narratives. Similarly, Killick and Boffey (2012) provide advice for foster parents to create stories for the children they are caring for, and these authors, amongst others, provide or suggest stories that can be used with children experiencing a range of challenges (e.g. Sunderland 2000).

The story is a universal form of expression. Story is present in most communication between us. We tell anecdotes, relive memories, recite jokes or relate our day-to-day experience to each other; humans are skilled storytellers. Therapeutic storytelling rests on this ancient practice. It is provided within the safety of a relationship between storyteller and listener. Stories provide a fictional world that we can visit together, 'A place that one can go to explore the difficulties that reality brings and to return stronger and more confident' (Killick and Boffey 2012, p.2).

Stories to aid healing use therapeutic metaphors based on the therapist's understanding of the experience of the other. Such stories are written with empathy. Margot Sunderland (2000), for example, compares such stories to allegorical tales such as the well-known Aesop's Fables. These tales are harsh and judgmental. They may teach, but they are unlikely to heal. Therapeutic stories are both more empathic and more hopeful. This sharing of a story builds trust in the relationship; the client feels known and understood by the other. In addition, new insight and renewed hope can be given through the power of the narrative. As Thomas and Killick (2007) point out, the story can express the inner lives, thoughts, feelings and motivations of the other as understood by the therapist, but without this being experienced as a personal intrusion. In this way stories can 'both describe and shape people's lives' (Freeman *et al.* 1997, p.47).

Story uses a language that we can all share. It is especially helpful for exploring feelings with children. Margot Sunderland (2000) points out that the language of feeling for children is not our everyday language but one that involves images, metaphors and stories. In using stories with children we are meeting them where they feel most comfortable, in the realm of imagination rather than cognition. As Sunderland writes: 'A therapeutic story can act as an "admission ticket" into a child's inner world' (Sunderland 2000, p.10).

Storytelling can be especially helpful for children living away from their birth families; these children can be too uncomfortable with direct approaches, but within the story they can tolerate thinking about their experience at one removed, whilst they are developing stronger relationships and safer ways of being within the family they now live with (Cattanach 2008; Killick and Boffey 2012). In this way children can be helped to integrate their past experience with their current experience. The story can help parents provide some compensation for what was missed within the child's early experience. A parent can use a claiming narrative, for example, to tell and show the child how they would have cared for them as a baby. The child gets an experience of being cherished as a baby through the storytelling process.

Storytelling is therefore a helpful process to facilitate mental health and emotional wellbeing. 'Stories are a very ancient way of soothing and calming and talking to the imaginative mind, providing new and more useful imagination, uncoupling the old associations and putting in place new, more positive ones...' (Parkinson 2009, p.52). As children engage and empathize with the characters and the story, they also connect with their own inner conflicts, thus finding solutions that they probably would not reach in other circumstances. The story has built in sufficient distance to help the children discover that they are not alone, and to consider different perspectives, leading to alternative solutions to their problems (Malchiodi and Ginns-Gruenberg 2008; Moore 2012). By working at this safe distance children are able to stay with feelings which cause them pain or distress. Instead of hiding or running from this experience they can spend the time needed to really think about what they are experiencing (Sunderland 2000).

Systemic interventions such as DDP work with the whole family. In fact, within DDP there is a particular emphasis on working with the parents before working with the child. This helps the parents receive support, achieve different understanding and gain strength so that they can remain available to their child as he goes on his own therapeutic journey. The therapist will consider with the parents the impact the child is having upon them, and how this impact is influenced by past relationships. The parent experiences an intersubjective relationship with the therapist, and learns first hand the power of PACE to give them a profound experience of being important to and understood by someone else. As the parents come to understand their own experience more deeply, they are better able to be attuned, available and responsive to their child. Their parenting becomes more deeply connected to their child's emotional experience whilst continuing to provide the structure, supervision and boundaries that the child needs. As with children, this is a process of sharing and developing stories; and as with children, creating stories for parents can be a useful way of giving them some distance from which they can explore their own parenting. In the process the parent is also developing her capacity to be mind-minded, able to enter imaginatively into the child's inner world of thoughts, feelings, beliefs, worries and desires. This facilitates a deep emotional connection with the child so necessary for the unconditional relationships a child needs to experience, to be accepted 'no matter what'. Mind-minded parenting helps parents to meet this need and so allows healing from the trauma experienced early in life.

Stories are part of being human; whether formal or informal, we are all storytellers. Traumatized children and their parents, however, cannot always give voice to these stories. '[O]ur childhoods leave in us...stories we never found a way to voice because no-one helped us to find the words. When we cannot find a way of telling our story, our story tells us, we dream these stories, we develop symptoms, or we find ourselves acting in ways we don't understand' (Grosz 2013, p.10). The challenges of parenting these children can lead to stories hardened in pain and rejection and limited by despair and challenge. Together we can create new stories based on multiple perspectives and touched by the hope that can come from support. Stories, as Jennings (2004) writes, are safe structures to help with anxieties and burdens. As these anxieties are externalized within the narrative construction, the burden can be lightened. In this way therapists can help their clients to move away from attitudes, beliefs and thinking that is unproductive and limiting to a more reflective stance infused with humour, imagination, curiosity and renewal (Parkinson 2009). Stories, as part of the therapeutic process, can change families' lives; the children's challenges and difficulties may continue, but family members can find a way of living together that over time will build security and help children to reach a state of peace with their past.

2

'Once Upon a Time...'
Creating Your Own Helping Stories

Introduction

Once upon a time there were two parents caring for their first child. They were kind and loving and the child, a daughter, had everything her heart desired. She grew in strength, wisdom and beauty, but these parents were not content. They wanted to give their child everything she needed, and they feared that one thing was missing. They had no stories for her; oh, they did read to her, shared with her the lovely story books written for children of her age, but none of these were created especially for her. They feared that they were letting her down by not finding a story that was hers alone. One day their distress at this state of affairs reached a climax; their daughter was beginning to fret as she picked up her parents' distress, and so they knew they had to do something. One of the parents decided that he would go out into the world and hunt for her story. He packed a small bag of provisions and, with a last look back at his partner and their child, he set off. Over the next few weeks he travelled far and wide, searching for this story. He came to many strange and wonderful places and he met many people. All the time he would ask the people he met if they knew the story created for his daughter. These were kind people and they could see the distress in this father's eyes. They searched their minds for the stories that they knew, hoping that one of these would be the story he was seeking, but no, the story created especially for his precious daughter remained elusive. He began to despair. He wanted to get back to his family, but he could not return empty-handed. At last, tired and foot weary, he entered an inn and ordered a light supper. The inn was very crowded as it was festival time in the town, and so he struggled to find a seat. He squeezed into the only seat remaining at a table already occupied by another man. They sat in companionable silence as each consumed his meal, and then struck up conversation over a final drink. Soon, as it was never far from his mind, the father told of his quest and wondered if this companion might know where he could find the story he was seeking. The companion asked him about his daughter. The father told of her intelligence and her beauty. He shared the things that made him and his partner laugh; the little things she might say and do. He shared the struggles of protecting a small child determined to test her independence. He told the story of her coming to them as a foundling child and how precious and vulnerable she seemed when she arrived with nothing but a blanket left with her by some unknown birth mother. As the sun set on the town, the father talked with delight about this daughter who was so close to his heart whilst his companion listened, nodding occasionally in encouragement. Finally the father returned to his quest and how it had brought him to this town on this night, but how his heart longed to return to his home and his family. The companion looked at him with kindness in his eyes. He gently touched the father on the arm and told him: "Go home, they are waiting for you. You have found the story you have been looking for, you need search no more." And so the father returned home, understanding at last that his daughter's story had been with him all along.

This is a whimsical story that I wrote for fun to open this chapter on creating stories. It is a reminder that we are all story creators; this is not something we need to learn to do. I therefore hesitate to give advice about how to create stories, as I believe it is in you already, although you will have different levels of confidence in how you use your creative potential. Stories can be simple or complex; short or long; anecdotal or more metaphorical; told, acted or written. Just sit where people meet together and you will hear stories all around you; to be human is to tell stories.

I have a very early memory of my grandmother; unfortunately she died when I was still very young, and so this memory is precious to me. She had a picture hanging on her wall that I had taken an interest in. It was a simple landscape; I think it was a house in a rural landscape. My grandmother took down the picture and sat me on her lap. She then made up a story inspired by the picture. Sadly I don't remember the story, but the act of telling stays with me. Many years later I watched as my father sat his young grandson on his lap and told him stories. He invented a character, Troublesome Tommy, and regaled my young son with the exploits of this lively lad. Each trip to the grandparents was an opportunity for grandfather and grandson to share another 'Tommy story'. Back home and I am out walking the dogs with my small daughter and a friend's son. We are busy hunting for dragons, creeping up on the tussocks of grass to see if we can find these elusive creatures; a more active storymaking than our usual 'story tree' where my children and I sit on the way home from school, making up stories for each other, generations of story creation that my now adult children continue to enjoy. Whilst writing this chapter my son has been enjoying creating a story as dungeon master for his 'Dungeons & Dragons' weekend with his friends, and my daughter has been meeting with a group to develop plots ready for NaNoWriMo (National Novel Writing Month).

Are we an unusual family in our abilities to create stories? I don't think so. I do think, however, that we were lucky in having early experiences that gave us confidence in our story-creating abilities. I have therefore included this chapter to hopefully give you the same confidence.

By helping stories I mean stories that have been written with a purpose that is more than entertainment. The purpose is to provide some helpful advice, guidance or understanding that the receiver of the story can use in his own life. Whether you are a parent or a practitioner, stories can be an important part of your caring for children and, indeed, for other adults. I hope that the stories included in this book will give you some inspiration to make your own stories. For the less confident amongst you I give some advice to help you with your own adventures into story creation.

Stimulating your creativity

For some people, creating stories comes easily; for others, it takes a little more effort. In the next section I provide some ideas for planning stories, but before you get to this stage you need an idea. Different people come to storymaking in different ways; some think in words, others in pictures; some start with characters, whilst others imagine the plot and then work back to the characters.

When I am working with a child I often get an image in my mind. As you read through the stories later in this book you will meet some of these – a child on a raft in a river (Story 17); a mother and daughter looking at each other across a ravine (Story 5); a cuckoo in a clock endlessly singing (Story 11). Each image resonates with something I understand about the child, and this then leads to the development of the story.

At other times the child might do or say something that gives me the idea for a character. For example, a child playing a game about a caterpillar that would not change into a butterfly (Story 1), or a child telling me tales about himself as a superhero (Story 4) – both inspired me to create a story around these characters. Finally, an action made by the child might be my starting point. A young man who cut himself before finally seeking help was my inspiration for 'Born to Care' (Story 7).

There are techniques that can be used to stimulate this creative process. For example, Sunderland (2000) suggests a strategy for identifying and better understanding the child's emotional experience. This involves imagining the child has drawn a picture or created a sand play sculpture of what it is like to be him in his life right now. By drawing the imagined picture or creating the sand play sculpture, you can listen to your imagination, allowing you to gain more insight into the child's experience than if you just relied on your more rational mind.

You might like to collect pictures, images from magazines, the internet, postcards and other sources. When you are thinking about creating the stories, these can be looked at as a source of inspiration. If you prefer to start with words, you could do a similar thing with a collection of words. Some bookshops sell sets of magnetic words that lend themselves to this purpose, although you might want to extend the range of words available.

Other people's stories can also provide inspiration. Reflecting on stories that have been written for children can lead to ideas for a story for the child you have in mind. Television programmes or films can similarly provide ideas that you can play with. Observing the animals and birds featured in a television series about Africa inspired me to write 'Survival of the Fittest' (Story 13), as there was something about the way the birds behaved that brought the experience of a child I knew to mind.

It can be fun to create stories together with a child. There is a range of ways you can do this. You might each take a turn in telling a story, or perhaps one of you starts the story and you take turns in adding to this. Killick and Boffey (2012) suggest asking a child to give a title, character, place and object and then you make up a story around these selections. They also suggest using props, for example having a bag of objects such as small toys, natural objects and pictures – the child chooses three to weave the story around. Storymaking cards can be used in the same way. You could use cards depicting places, people, creatures and objects. The child can select cards (e.g. one from each category) to make the story. A game can be made by drawing out cards or objects at random, and each person creating a story from these random selections. There are also story games for sale that include story cards and a board. Each person in turn places a picture on the board, and the story is built up around the pictures.

Structure of stories

All stories have a basic structure consisting of a beginning, middle and end.

- The beginning: This frames the story, introducing the setting, theme and main character.

- The middle: This is the journey of the story represented by plot and narrative. The action or events are described in a way that builds interest and some suspense.

- The end: The story comes to a resolution as the message of the story is conveyed.

Beyond this basic structure the development of the story will be shaped to some extent by the type of story and the reason for creating it. There is a range of story types that can be helpful for children and, to some extent, adults as well. Across this range the story creator needs to make some decisions about how realistic to make the story setting. For example, stories can be autobiographical as when families recall events or anecdotes based on their experience. Alternatively, they can be metaphorical, allowing one thing to substitute for another. For example, the image of an exploding bottle of pop can help a child understand the difficulties they can have when they try to avoid their feelings.

Different story types are explored in more detail next, but there are also some general thoughts about story creation. For example, Moore (2012) suggests that fantasy settings allow children to have some distance from the story, although older children and those who struggle imaginatively might do better with settings that are closer to real life. Even with these, however, the fictional element is important; if the story is too close to home, it might trigger a more defensive response. There are also decisions to be made about the perspective the story is written from. A first person perspective within which the main character is telling the story can feel more direct. Lacher *et al.* (2005) suggest that such narratives can be helpful when writing narratives that help children feel a sense of belonging in the family or to develop skills. On the other hand, the third person perspective in which the narrator tells events, feelings and characteristics of the main character can provide what Lacher and colleagues (2005) describe as a 'zone of safety', which can be more comfortable when dealing with emotional or trauma-related problems that children may experience.

Story types

Figure 2.1. Helping stories

Broadly, stories can be divided into two main styles depending upon how direct the story creator wants to be about the content of the story in relation to the person it is being written for.

BIOGRAPHICAL STORIES

If the story is about a real person, perhaps the person for whom the story is created, or someone she might know or be interested to hear about, then it can be described as biographical. If the storyteller is relating an incident or anecdote about herself, then it would be described as autobiographical. Some of the illustrative stories in this book are biographical. For example, in 'Born to Care' (Story 7), the story describes a boy growing up in foster care, and in 'William and Edward' (Story 17), the experiences of a mother and her adopted son. The most autobiographical story is 'A Daughter's Tale' (Story 16) in which I gave the child a voice to talk about her experience to her mother.

These stories can be created with some thought and attention, but biographical stories can also be woven into family life or therapeutic sessions. Relating incidents or anecdotes can be storytelling at its most spontaneous. Sharing memories or relating stories about people of particular relevance to the individual can be very helpful in the moment. Imagine, for example, talking with an individual about his experience of living in foster care. Perhaps this person had a grandfather who was evacuated during the war. Sharing the story of the grandfather's struggles and triumphs in this difficult situation might be particularly resonant for the individual's own struggles about being in foster care, and might give some hope that he, like his grandfather, can become stronger out of this experience.

Children often like to hear stories of their birth or when they were little, and this storytelling as part of family life can be an important part of forming their sense of self or identity. Sadly, for children in foster care or adopted homes, such anecdotes may be thin on the ground, but the families can still share memories of experiences they have known together as well as the sadness of the stories that have been missed because they did not know each other earlier in life. Some of the claiming narratives, as described below, can be particularly helpful for filling in such gaps as the child and parents share a fantasy of what it would have been like to have known the child at birth or as a young child.

Everyday life can also be shared in story form as a way of deepening the sharing of experience and of dealing with the struggles of life as they happen. Two examples illustrate what I mean. A parent shared with me the difficulty she was having in getting her young child to talk about his day at school. Frustrating question and monosyllabic answer sessions were getting her nowhere until she had the inspired idea to start with her day instead of interrogating the child. Over a drink and snack she would relate the story of her day, and following her cue, the child began to talk about his own day.

Dan Hughes, clinical psychologist and specialist in working with traumatized children, likes to relate stories of his granddaughter during his training. I love his story of the meltdown this little girl had in the supermarket one day. At Alice's request, her fraught mother related to her the story of the meltdown. Starting with 'One day a little girl called Alice...', she related the whole episode in story form. This helped Alice to recover from this emotionally overwhelming experience. Alice loved it, and wanted the story over and over again as she processed the experience. Alice was able to understand her experience in a way that was not shame-inducing, and that increased her security with her mother. This is a gentle way of spontaneously using stories, sometimes at the most difficult of moments, which I have passed on to some of the parents I have worked with.

METAPHORICAL STORIES

Metaphor can be used for a more indirect story. Sometimes it can be easier to hear and relate to a story that is not directly focused upon the listener or reader. If the issues within the story are uncomfortable, painful or even distressing, it can lead to a defensive response, especially when this is 'close to home'. The use of metaphor can reduce this defensiveness and make the story more helpful to the individual. Metaphorical stories can also be very engaging, especially for younger children. Metaphors that resonate with the listener can be especially captivating. For example, the story of 'Connor, the Superhero' (Story 4) held the interest of the child it was created for as he had a particular fascination with superheroes.

A metaphor is a way of talking or writing that uses an image, animate or inanimate object or story to represent something else. Many of the illustrative stories included in this book are metaphorical. For example, the children are represented by characters such as a dog, a mermaid, a space boy, and even a cuckoo clock and a balloon; the dilemmas or worries are represented by experiences such as not wanting to change from a caterpillar to a butterfly, hiding beneath a superhero cloak or trying to cross a river. Finally, the resolutions are represented by being helped to achieve some change such as transforming, healing, getting across something or feeling noticed.

As well as these two main styles, stories can be divided into a range of types, although these are not separate categories. As many of the stories in this book illustrate, a story can reflect one or more of these types.

SOLUTION STORIES

These are quite solution-focused in their content, and give advice to help someone cope with a problem, dilemma or issue facing them. The story I have written at the beginning of this chapter is an example of such a solution story. This example is used to explore a way of planning this type of story. (A template for such story planning can be found in Appendix 1.)

Planning a solution story

Theme, emotional problem experienced	The theme is creating a story for a child. The message is that we can all create stories. It is metaphorical – a physical journey to represent the imagination.
The setting	A simple, fairy tale-type setting, with not too much detail. It conveys a journey through a changing landscape. Has an old-fashioned feel to it.
Main character or characters (hero or protagonist)	Parents, with one parent going in search of a story. The other parent and child remain behind, waiting for the father to return.
Theme, problem or challenge faced	The search for the right story for the child. The obstacle is that no one he meets knows the story he is seeking.
Helpers	The father meets a companion in an inn. This companion has wisdom, but does not give an answer; he helps the parent to find his own answer.
Are there any objects of special significance?	The journey the parent makes and the story he finally tells carries the significance.
The resolution	The parent discovers he already knows the story.
Prizes gained	The parent can go back home to his partner and child.

THERAPEUTIC STORIES

Helping stories all have a therapeutic element because they aim to provide help, advice or guidance for individuals with problems, issues or dilemmas. I have used the term 'helping stories' to distinguish these from the more targeted therapeutic stories which aim at helping to resolve specific emotional difficulties. These are also solution stories, but are created specifically to help with an emotional problem or issue. For example, 'Millie and Her Mother' (Story 5) describes the fear or distrust a child can experience when they have been hurt by parents, and the pain of rejection for the parent who tries to care for this child.

The story explores how the child can build trust to replace mistrust and accept the care of her mother.

Margot Sunderland (2000) writes the most beautiful therapeutic stories. She suggests that children are helped by these stories because the problem is expressed indirectly. The child's reality is represented symbolically because it is in a different context from the actual life circumstances of the child.

I use the example of 'Millie and Her Mother' to explore a way of planning this type of story. (A template for such story planning can be found in Appendix 2.)

Planning a therapeutic story

Theme, emotional problem experienced	Fear of being parented. The child struggling to trust a mother.
The setting	A ravine with a mother and child standing on the cliff edge, either side of the ravine.
Main character or characters (hero or protagonist)	A mother and a daughter.
How will the character encounter the problem?	The problem is represented by the distance between the mother and daughter and the ravine that separates them. The struggle is represented by two characters – Fear and Sad. There is externalization of what each is experiencing. The daughter copes by rejecting her mother. Self-reliance is the unhelpful coping strategy. The crisis is that they cannot be together.
Crisis to solution	A new character, Hope, appears to move the mother and daughter to a solution. The solution is represented by removing Fear and Sad who find they no longer need the mother and daughter.
The resolution	The daughter learns to trust the mother and they can finally be together. The daughter experiences herself as loveable and the mother as always loving her.

TRAUMA STORIES

These are less focused on finding a solution to a problem, dilemma or emotional issue and more about helping people with the experience of trauma. The story about 'Kirsty, the Cuckoo in the Nest' (Story 2) is an example of such a story in that it explores the trauma of being hurt in a family and having to move more than once from different families. This story also illustrates the overlapping nature of these story types as it also has elements of life story and of therapeutic story.

Lacher and colleagues (2005) suggest that trauma stories are useful for individuals who have experienced trauma in their lives because they can help with processing this experience; the story helps the individual to make sense of his experience and allow it to become integrated into his sense of who he is.

The example of 'Kirsty, the Cuckoo in the Nest' is used to explore a way of planning this type of story. (A template for such story planning can be found in Appendix 3.)

Planning a trauma story

Theme, trauma experienced	A mother giving up a child to foster care and then adoption.
The setting	In a wood.
Main character or characters (hero or protagonist)	The main character is a cuckoo. Her journey from a bird family to a foster bird family to an adoptive bird family is described. This mirrors the life experience of the child. The adoptive family is represented by a different bird family.
Making sense	The cuckoo experiences the life story as mirrored by the birds. The behaviour of these birds shows the ambivalence of the cuckoo in being part of the family, and her need for self-reliance.
Helpers	A wise owl helps the mummy and daddy birds to take care of the cuckoo. This wise owl helps the cuckoo with her fears.

cont.

Planning a trauma story *cont.*

The resolution	The cuckoo learns to enjoy being close to her parents, but also that she can be supported when she does not feel like being close. Unconditional love is offered and accepted, and the cuckoo and mummy bird learn to fly together.

LIFE STORIES

These are stories to support life story understanding. As Killick and Boffey (2012) suggest, we all like personal and family stories. These can be in the form of short anecdotes, memories of experiences child or family members have been through or historical stories about relatives or ancestors. These stories help to form part of our identity, and the storying of our life is a continuing process that we engage in as children and throughout adulthood: 'To not know these stories is to not know part of ourselves' (Killick and Boffey 2012, p.49). Part of exploring life story is gaining a sense of belonging within the family. This can be challenging for children who have had to move family. 'Survival of the Fittest' (Story 13) is an example of a story that explores life experience alongside the exploration of sibling relationships. The metaphor of the Shoebill birds provides a way of reflecting on the real-life experience of two brothers whilst also providing some hope that a different life experience is now possible.

Lacher *et al.* (2005) identify claiming narratives as being a helpful way of helping these children to understand that they should have been loved and cherished, and to gain an experience of now being loved and cherished. Additionally they suggest developmental narratives to help children explore imaginatively experiences missed earlier in life.

The example of 'Survival of the Fittest' is used to explore a way of planning this type of story. (A template for such story planning can be found in Appendix 4.)

Planning a narrative to explore life story

Theme, life experience being explored	The experience of growing up with parents who are neglectful and frightening. Two brothers, one marginally favoured. Moving to adoption. Sibling relationship.
The setting	Set in Africa and the habits of two types of birds. Includes the habits of these birds to mirror the differences between families.
Main character or characters (hero or protagonist)	Shoebills and Hamerkops to represent two families. The Shoebill brothers come to live with the Hamerkop parents.
Fear and hope	The parenting of the Hamerkops tailored to the needs of the strong and the weak brother illustrates the fear of not being special by the strong bird that perceives the weak brother as becoming the favourite. Hope comes from the parents going to find the strong brother when he runs away.
Helpers	A neighbouring bird witnesses the brothers fighting and offers to help. She helps the parents to help the strong brother.
The resolution	The strong brother returns to the family and the parents support him, even when the old worries surface.

INSIGHT STORIES

These are stories to increase understanding and to gain a sense of hope and possibility. Many stories written for adults will be aimed at providing increased insight. Thus 'William and Edward' (Story 17) and 'Longing and Belonging' (Story 18) are two stories written to help practitioners provide support to parents who might be struggling to provide empathy and acceptance for their children.

For children, successful narratives, as described by Lacher *et al.* (2005), can provide a sense of who the children are, what has happened to them and who they might become. Such narratives can guide behaviour, understand values and provide support and encouragement.

'A Mummy Finds Out How to Look After Her Baby' (Story 14) is written as an insight story, with elements of a successful narrative for a child who was struggling to understand how her foster mother could care for her when her birth mother could not. This story gave the child hope that she could become a child who was cared for.

The example of 'Longing and Belonging' is used to explore a way of planning this type of story. (A template for such story planning can be found in Appendix 5.)

Planning an insight story

Theme, insight being offered	The theme is the importance of acceptance. Sometimes we can't change the child, but through acceptance, the child is helped and change might then happen.
The setting	The main setting is a river, with a child stranded on a raft in the fast-running water.
Main character or characters (hero or protagonist)	A birth mother appears briefly, but the main characters are an adoptive mother and father and their daughter.
The problem	The daughter longs for her first mother and fears belonging within her new family. The mother tries lots of ways to help her daughter feel she belongs, represented by leaving the raft and coming to the shore.
Helpers	Wisdom, a character that is the externalized wisdom the mother already has.
The resolution	The mother joins the child on the raft, accepting her need not to belong, but supporting her anyway. She allows her to express her biggest fears and have these accepted. This acceptance allows the raft to float to the shore where the father waits for them.

Conclusion

I hope that the ideas in this chapter give you the confidence to create your own stories to use in parenting, therapy, direct work or life story work, stories that can help the children you care for experience more deeply, in more integrative ways, and thus bring healing. You will almost certainly find your own way of doing this, your own stimulation for your creativity, but this chapter may give you some starting points. Above all else, enjoy the process of story creation and the connections with others that creating stories can give you.

> And so the father returned to his daughter and he took her in his arms and told her the story that was in his heart and in his mind. She snuggled into him, looking up into his deep brown eyes. She listened to his words and felt his love and security. Deep within her grew a sense of belonging, of knowing she had parents who would love and care for her no matter what. She grew up experiencing the safety of parents who would always make it okay, however difficult things were, and the joy of unconditional love, no matter what mistakes she made. Though she tested these many times during her childhood, they remained a foundation that she could always return to. Eventually she left home, found her own partner and had children of her own. She knew the stories in her heart and mind and was able to give her children their stories also. And so it is fair to say that they all lived happily ever after.

Part I

LOOKING BACK AND MOVING ON

LIFE IN STORIES

Story 1

The Caterpillar That Did Not Want to Become a Butterfly

Story type: Life story; Therapeutic

Themes: Exploring life story; Thinking with children about transitions; Exploring the range of feelings moving can evoke

Age range: 4–8 years

Stories can be a useful resource to help children make sense of their past experience and any changes that they are facing in the present. Many of the stories in this book have a life story element to them. The stories in this part have been written explicitly to help children in care or who have been adopted to make sense of transition and permanence.

Sadly, children living in care can have a number of changes of family once they have been removed from their birth family. Not only do they have to cope with loss and separation from their birth parents, they then move between foster carers or from foster care into adoption or some other permanent arrangement. Loss piles on top of loss. When these arrangements also break down it is difficult for the children to believe in the idea of permanence. I remember one little girl who had experienced a number of foster placements, a failed adoption and was moving to yet another set of foster carers. The social worker asked me how she might help this little girl understand that she was moving again. This was not the challenge; the difficulty would be how to help the girl understand when she was staying!

Not only do children have to cope with moving from family to family, they also have to make sense of why this keeps happening. It is unusual for children to grasp the idea that their parents have failed to look after them properly. Instead they tend to look to themselves. They must be bad, or naughty; something is wrong with them. This becomes a very uncomfortable legacy to live with. The children wait in fear of moving again. The inevitability of moving becomes firmly linked with the certainty of their own badness. Unconditional love and acceptance have not been available to these children, and therefore the idea that they can be loved no matter what is also not an experience that they can understand or believe in.

The children expect to move – sometimes patiently, but with resignation; sometimes with rage and anger. Some children escalate their behaviour to hasten the ending – moving is better than waiting to move; endings are an uncomfortable and distressing fact of their lives. Some children want to move often, not staying anywhere long enough to be truly known; others want to stay and fear moving on. Transition becomes part of their life story, and permanence is an unknown possibility.

The little girl who inspired this first story had coped with many moves before she was six. This was too many moves for a little girl to manage, especially following a year of severe neglect with her birth parents. She had settled well in her latest short-term foster placement. These foster carers understood her and dealt well with the challenges she presented. Finally, a long-term foster placement was identified, and the foster carers were asked to prepare this little girl for one more move. As they talked to her about moving on to a 'forever family' she appeared not to understand. She stubbornly ignored these conversations and gave every indication that she meant to stay.

Whilst this little girl could not talk about her fears or anxieties, she was able to communicate with me through her play. She initiated a game that conveyed to me her desire to stay where she was. She asked me to play 'caterpillars' with her. In this game of her devising she was a caterpillar, hiding from me. Even though I found her and 'fed' her she would not change into a butterfly. She wanted to play this over and over, showing me in the only way that she could that she would not transform. If only this little girl could stay where she was – but a move was imminent. I decided to write the story of the caterpillar game, using it to explain that a change must happen, but also conveying some hope that with lots of help she would be able to move and settle with a new family.

The Caterpillar That Did Not Want to Become a Butterfly

Once upon a time there was a little caterpillar called Angela. She was an unusual caterpillar, because as you know, most caterpillars are green or brown, but Angela wasn't green or brown. She was pink. Everyone thought she was the most beautiful caterpillar in the world.

Angela the caterpillar liked to play and she liked to eat. She especially loved to eat tasty green plants. Sometimes she hid, and she loved being found. When Angela was eating or playing or hiding she was a happy caterpillar.

Sometimes, however, Angela was a sad and confused caterpillar. She was especially sad and confused when she thought about changing. Angela was clever. She knew all about caterpillars turning into butterflies. She knew that one day she would be wrapped up in a cocoon and that she would nibble her way out and become a butterfly.

Angela did not like this idea at all. She wanted to always be a caterpillar. Angela decided that she would be a caterpillar that did not turn into a butterfly. So Angela continued to play, and to eat and to hide. She grew bigger and bigger. Soon she was a big, pink caterpillar, but she did not turn into a butterfly.

Now Angela would like her story to end here. She wants to be the caterpillar that doesn't turn into a butterfly. Caterpillars can't stay the same. This story does not end here. Here's what happens to Angela the caterpillar.

Angela the caterpillar had friends and family that loved her very much. Angela had lived in lots of different families, and she had had lots of mummies and daddies. Angela the caterpillar liked these families. She liked to play and eat and hide with these families. However, when Angela was feeling sad or confused or angry, she wanted to be alone.

One day Angela was very sad and confused and angry. She did not want to be a butterfly and have to live in another family. She did not want to get to know another mummy and daddy. Angela ran away and hid.

Now young caterpillars cannot stay hidden. They need family and friends to look after them. Luckily Angela had lots of family and friends to help her. She had a 'for now' mummy and daddy, Karen and Chris, who loved her very much. They wanted to help Angela the caterpillar. They looked and looked, and guess what? They found her!

Angela the caterpillar was glad to be found. She was feeling lonely. But she was also feeling very cross. She shouted and pulled faces. She broke her toys. She tried to run away again.

Karen and Chris did not get cross with Angela the caterpillar. They sat with her and told her that they knew she was feeling scared and that she did not want to become a butterfly. They would help her. They remembered when they had become butterflies. It was exciting, but it was also scary.

Angela also had a friend, a beautiful blue butterfly called Phyllis. Phyllis had known Angela the caterpillar since she was a small pale caterpillar. She had watched her grow big and strong, and very pink.

Phyllis knew that Angela the caterpillar needed a very special mummy and daddy to help her become a butterfly. She needed a mummy and daddy butterfly who knew all about helping caterpillars who felt sad and cross and scared.

Phyllis looked and looked and found just the right mummy and daddy butterfly.

Now Angela the caterpillar had lots of butterflies to help her. She still did not want to become a butterfly, but she was getting very big. She could not stay as a caterpillar. She wanted to hide again, but her friends and family said, "Don't hide Angela, we will help you."

Phyllis the blue butterfly said, "Don't hide Angela, I will help you."

The new mummy and daddy butterfly said, "Don't hide Angela, we will help you too."

And do you know what? With all this help, Angela did not feel so sad or cross or scared.

Angela the caterpillar became Angela, the most beautiful pink butterfly in the world.

Angela the butterfly still sometimes feels sad or cross or scared, but all her butterfly friends and family are there to help her. Angela the butterfly has grown big and strong, and is a very beautiful butterfly indeed.

Story 2

Kirsty, the Cuckoo in the Nest

Story type: Trauma; Life story

Themes: Exploring life story; Fears of moving on again; Learning to live with a family; Coping with sadness; Developing self-reliance

Age range: 5–9 years

For many children, moving on to a new family is very challenging, but learning to stay with a family can be just as difficult.

Children find it hard to settle and feel secure within a family when their previous experience has been of trauma, loss and separation. The children have a hard time making sense of what has happened to them, and learning to trust that it won't happen again. Small events within the new family can trigger major stress and insecurity.

For example, it is not uncommon for children to fear that very normal family life experiences are a sign that they are going to be sent away. They therefore have very little tolerance for negative experiences within the family – being told off, a parent giving attention to a sibling or even something as simple as a nice day out coming to an end. In other words, the children are left with chronic fears of abandonment. They are fine as long as they are getting what they want, things are calm and parents are being attentive to them. They cannot tolerate the frustration of being told 'no'; they don't want to experience even mild negative feelings; worry, sadness, anxiety and being 'in trouble' create huge panic, panic that stems from the belief that one day they will have to leave this family too.

Fearing rejection, it is not uncommon when they meet these frustrations for the children to reject first. They push their parents away; they run away and become angry. At the extreme they try to hurt themselves or others. These behaviours are very difficult to live with; parents are doing their best to look after the children with nurture, warmth and appropriate boundaries, but however hard they try, normal family experiences lead to major meltdowns. These patterns of behaviour wear the families out, and understandably, parents become frustrated. They wonder what they are doing wrong or what they could do differently. Eventually they struggle to remain empathic towards the children. Their love for their child keeps them going, but it is difficult to like the child on a day-to-day basis. Hughes and Baylin (2012) describe the state of 'blocked care' that parents can enter into in these situations. Parenting becomes a chore, with little satisfaction or joy left. The child's anxieties increase as the parents struggle in these ways, and the family is on a treadmill of fear and despair.

Sometimes foster and adoptive children will have fantasies about their birth parents, imagining that they have been kidnapped or that their birth parents would treat them differently. In my experience this often focuses on the mother. The child develops a longing to be with an idealized mother and finds it even harder to tolerate the ups and downs of family life. The poor foster or adoptive mother in the meantime has to cope with not measuring up to an impossible standard. It is hard not to experience a sense of failure when you are continually told you are not doing a good job!

At the bottom of all this difficult experience is confusion for the children. They are not sure what has happened to them, why they have had the experiences they have had and, imagining that their own 'badness' is at the root of this, they hold an intense fear of the future. They live in the past and the future to such an extent that they can't relax and enjoy the present. The whole family needs support from practitioners who understand the impact of separation, loss and joining new families. An important part of this is helping the family to support the children in making sense of what has happened and is happening to them. Whilst this understanding won't make the fears go away, it can provide some hope that they may not always feel this way. Their experience is understandable, and this provides an alternative story to the story the children hold that says 'I am bad and nothing can change this'.

Life story work is part of helping the children make sense of this confusion. This is much more than a life story book that tells them the facts of their life; it is more an ongoing process of helping the children to discover what has been their experience and to make some sense of why. It provides an alternative narrative for the children to the one they have developed in their fear and confusion. Whilst this won't make the first narrative go away, just having alternatives can lead to more flexibility and hope. (The use of life story work is explored further in the introduction to Story 14.) Stories created with and/or for the children can be a helpful part of this process.

This next story is an example of this. It was inspired by my experience of a number of children who were removed from their parents at birth, lived in foster care and then moved into adoptive families. These children, whilst initially settling in with the family, found it very difficult when significant events happened which threatened their fragile security. A parent becoming ill, going away to work or needing to give more attention to an ailing family member are all experiences that secure children will manage but that can rock the foundations of a child who is already feeling insecure. I wrote the story of the cuckoo for a little girl who found it very hard to accept that her adoptive mother would not leave her. Even when things were going well, this little girl tried to be self-reliant, to not need her mother. She could not tolerate any small negative experiences, and would become very angry and rejecting of her mother at these times.

Kirsty, the Cuckoo in the Nest

This is a story about a cuckoo called Kirsty. She lives in the wood. Kirsty is happy with her family, but it wasn't always so. This is a story about how Kirsty learned to live with her family.

Kirsty's birth mother had had a hard life. She moved from nest to nest, always struggling to find things to eat. Sometimes she ate things that made her poorly. When she knew she was going to have a chick, she was worried. She could not look after herself, so how would she look after a chick as well? She confided this to a wise cuckoo that also lived in the wood. The wise cuckoo agreed that it would not be a good idea for Kirsty's mother to look after a chick.

The wise cuckoo told her about another bird family that could help. They were not cuckoos but they were very kind. They would look after Kirsty until a permanent family could be found. Kirsty's mother felt sad, but thought that this was for the best. She flew through the woods and laid her egg in the nest of this kind bird family.

Kirsty hatched out and the family took good care of her. Kirsty lived with this family for quite some time. She enjoyed being with them. She had brothers and sisters and a mother and father to look after her. Kirsty wanted to stay with them forever. But this was not possible. There were other birds that needed a family, and Kirsty needed her own 'forever' family.

This was hard for Kirsty; she had to move to another nest. She had a new mother and father and a new brother and sister. They told her that they would be her forever family, but Kirsty did not know what this meant. They were a kind and patient family and they took good care of Kirsty. They made sure she was safe; they fed her and helped her to get really good at flying. Kirsty began to relax, and even started to enjoy being with her family. But one day something awful happened. Mummy bird became poorly and went away. Kirsty did not know what to think. She did not know where Mummy bird was. She did not think she was going to come back. She stayed very close to Daddy bird. Kirsty did not think she would see Mummy bird again.

Mummy bird did get better and she came home. Kirsty was frightened. She did not want to lose another mother. This was such a scary thought that Kirsty decided there and then that she would learn not to need a mother any more. She turned her back on her.

Kirsty would go flying, but she made sure that Mummy bird did not come too. She enjoyed flying all on her own. Flying helped her to forget how hard she was working not to need a mother.

Mummy bird tried to help Kirsty. She did not get cross and she showed Kirsty her kind face. She noticed what Kirsty was doing, and let her know that she was there if she was needed. Sometimes when Kirsty was flying she would notice Mummy bird just a little way away. Kirsty would fly a little closer and then away again. Kirsty wasn't sure she wanted Mummy bird close, but sometimes it felt nice that Mummy was nearby. This made Mummy bird and Kirsty feel happy. They noticed that it was easier to be a bit closer when they were happy.

They could not always be happy, though. Sometimes Kirsty was naughty and Mummy bird had to tell her off. Both Mummy bird and Kirsty felt anxious at these times. Kirsty remembered that she must not need her mother, and she would get mad at her. She jumped up and down and hissed and spat. Then she would go off and fly on her own again. It was hard for Kirsty and Mummy bird to feel happy again. Sometimes Daddy bird tried to help too; this was a little easier. But Daddy bird did not like to see Kirsty being angry with Mummy bird, and they all felt cross and bothered.

Now there lived in the wood a wise owl called Ollie. (Her name was Olivetta, but she liked to be called Ollie for short.) Ollie noticed that Kirsty wasn't happy and she wanted to help Mummy and Daddy bird talk to her. Ollie thought that Kirsty did want to be happy with Mummy and Daddy bird and her brother and sister, but it was so hard. When she felt happy she felt closer to Mummy bird, but this frightened her. She did not want to need her mother. She would get angry and stubborn. This helped her to feel in charge again. She was lonely but it felt a little bit safer. Ollie explained this to Mummy and Daddy bird. They felt very sad for Kirsty.

Ollie helped Mummy and Daddy bird take care of Kirsty in a way that helped her to feel safer. Sometimes Kirsty would become a little chick again, and Mummy and Daddy bird would look after her. Kirsty liked being taken care of. Kirsty would go flying with Mummy bird. She enjoyed these times together, but sometimes it felt too much, and Kirsty would go off on her own again.

Sometimes Kirsty felt sad. She did not want to feel sad. Feeling sad made her need her mother and she did not want to need her mother. Ollie was very patient. She told Kirsty that she knew how hard this was. So scary to need your mother, so scary to think you might lose your mother again. Kirsty would cuddle in to her mother, but she covered her ears. She did not want to hear Mummy bird tell her that she loved her. Mummy bird was patient and kind too. She let Kirsty know that it was all right. She would stay close by. She would keep an eye on her. She would love her and keep her safe. Even when Kirsty was cross, even when Kirsty did not want her to be close, even when Kirsty tried to make her go away – Mummy bird would stay close by so that Kirsty would not be alone. She would keep Kirsty safe and Kirsty would not feel so frightened all the time.

Gradually with Mummy and Daddy bird and Ollie's support, Kirsty's fear subsided. She realized that she really did want to figure out how to enjoy being close to Mummy bird. Sometimes she still got scared and pushed her away, but Ollie would be there quietly and patiently supporting them, and Mummy bird stayed strong, even when Kirsty was angry and distant. Daddy bird helped too. He helped them both to be strong.

Mummy bird and Kirsty learned to fly together. They were both stronger this way. They were a true mother and daughter. Slowly Kirsty learned not to be frightened any more. She learned that it was okay when things went wrong. She learned that she was loved whether she was happy, sad, cross or worried.

Finally, Kirsty was a cuckoo in the nest that loved to live with her family.

Story 3

The Puppy That Needed Healing

Story type: Therapeutic; Life story

Themes: Moving families; Developing self-reliance; Learning to get help with hurts

Age range: 4–8 years

Children who have been neglected early in life learn not to expect care and attention. Children are born with an instinct to elicit care from their parents or caregivers. Very early in life they signal their need for comfort. When children repeatedly experience these signals being ignored, they learn to override this instinct. They stop signalling their needs.

Unfortunately this learning goes very deep; it becomes biological as this behaviour pattern becomes wired into the brain. When these children move to foster or adoptive homes they therefore continue to hide rather than signal their needs. The expression 'Once bitten, twice shy' fits very well for these children. They have learned a very painful lesson, which is that they are not going to be looked after. It is even more painful to keep seeking this care when it isn't forthcoming, and so they protect themselves by no longer looking for comfort or help.

Different children make sense of this in different ways, but they rarely believe that their birth parents were at fault. Much more typically, children view themselves as deficient in some way – not good enough, not worthy of care. This very core belief then drives their future behaviour. Even though care is now on offer, the children do not see this. To protect themselves from anticipated neglect they no longer test out whether parents are available to meet their needs. They cannot learn that things are now different. They continue behaving in response to their earliest beliefs.

This development of self-reliance is explored further in Part III, revealing the extremes that this can lead to. In this story a simpler view of self-reliance is explored. This story was inspired by a number of young children who try and hide away their pain or discomfort but who can be very cross as a consequence.

The Puppy That Needed Healing

Once upon a time there was a puppy dog called Jasmine. She was a lovely dog with silky ears and a long pretty tail. Everyone thought that she was very pretty, although Jasmine wasn't so sure about this. She lived on a farm with her mum, dad and litter brother, Casper. Jasmine was a lively puppy that knew what she wanted. Sometimes this got her into trouble with her mum and dad who thought she was a bit stubborn.

The farmer looked after all the dogs, but sometimes he forgot about them, and then they would be hungry. Jasmine's mum and dad would go off to try and find some food, but they, too, sometimes forgot their puppies. It seemed that no one was looking after Jasmine and Casper.

Sometimes Jasmine and Casper went off on their own. They liked to explore, and sometimes they even found some food to eat. One day when they were out, Jasmine and Casper came across another dog. He was not very friendly; Jasmine and Casper ran away from him. Whilst they were running, Jasmine stumbled and hurt herself on some glass. It hurt a lot. Jasmine didn't know what to do.

She went into the barn and curled up in the straw, hoping it would get better. She did not want to tell anyone about it because she thought they might be cross with her. She curled up tight and stayed in the barn. Gradually it did seem to get better. Soon there was not even a scar where the wound had been. What Jasmine didn't realize was that it hadn't fully healed. A splinter of glass stayed deep inside. Jasmine tried to forget about it but sometimes it would start to hurt again and she could not ignore it.

The two puppies grew older. It was time to leave their mum and dad. The farmer found new owners for the puppies. Jasmine and Casper were very lucky because the new owners wanted to keep them both. They moved to the new house. Sometimes Jasmine would miss the farm, but she liked having her own basket to sleep in and, oh, the bliss of getting plenty of food. Their owners were very kind and kept them safe. Both Jasmine and Casper were able to grow big and strong. Even though things were so much better for Jasmine, the old hurt did not go away; on some days, the glass splinter within Jasmine would really bother her. She tried to ignore it but this was difficult, and she would get very cross. Casper couldn't talk to Jasmine when she was cross. He didn't know what was wrong. He stayed away from her and she felt very lonely. And this just made her crosser.

There was an older dog, also living with them, who worried about Jasmine. She was a collie dog with gentle eyes; Jasmine liked being with her. Sometimes the collie dog tried to help her. She seemed to know that Jasmine had a splinter inside and she wanted to help Jasmine to make it better. Jasmine didn't like this and decided to keep away. The collie understood this. She didn't push Jasmine.

The collie was a wise dog. She knew that Jasmine didn't want her to help with the splinter, but she also knew that it wouldn't heal on its own; it would carry on making Jasmine cross. She was very patient with Jasmine. She didn't get cross that Jasmine didn't want to see her. She liked Jasmine and kept an eye on her. She talked to Jasmine's owners. The owners helped Jasmine. They helped the pain to feel better, but this wasn't enough to make the splinter go away. The collie worried when Jasmine was cross and worried how much the splinter was hurting Jasmine. She waited and waited until one day Jasmine was especially cross and bothered.

Jasmine came into the garden and started running around and around. She was feeling so cross she didn't know what to do. Then she noticed the collie watching her. This made her even crosser and she went up and barked at her. The collie didn't get cross but just looked at her with her kind old eyes. She let Jasmine know that she was thinking about her. Jasmine was feeling very tired by now and she just couldn't bark any more. Instead she went to the collie and curled up next to her. Very gently the collie licked her tummy. She was very careful and it helped just a little bit. Jasmine began to realize that the collie could help her, although sometimes she was still too frightened to let her. The owners, seeing what was happening, came over too. Slowly and quietly they also took care of Jasmine. They helped Casper to be patient, letting him know that his sister would play with him again when she was ready.

Gradually and patiently they were all able to help Jasmine heal. There were still some days when Jasmine felt frightened, and when she wouldn't let them near, but they learned to be patient. They waited until Jasmine was ready again. With this help, the splinter did work its way to the surface, and finally it fell out. Jasmine felt safe at last. She came skipping out into the garden feeling strong and well and happy. She went up to the collie and they had a good play together. Jasmine told the collie that she didn't think she needed any more healing. The collie smiled and agreed. She told Jasmine that she was now free to live her life as puppies were supposed to. Jasmine went to her owners and rolled on her back; laughing, they tickled her tummy. She fetched a ball and with a little play bow she dropped it at their feet. Casper ran up ready to play too. The owners threw the ball, and as brother and sister ran to fetch it, Jasmine felt glad that she had let the collie help her.

Notes about Part I

Whilst the stories in this part have been written about transition and permanence for foster and adopted children, these are not the only children who can be unsettled by instability. Parental divorce, step-parenting, hospitalization of a parent or even moving home or country can all give children an experience of transition, loss or disruption that can leave them emotionally confused and upset.

Adopted children can experience a range of fantasies about what life would be like if they lived with their birth family, although children actually living within their birth families are not immune to such fantasies. Children living with a separated family are at risk of idealizing the absent parent, imagining a better life with the parent. Children struggling with change and family upset might start to get a sense that they do not fit in with the family; they imagine that maybe they have been kidnapped, that somewhere there was another family where they would fit in better. They fantasize about what it would be like if they could find this family. Displacement and instability can lead to a need to create an inner world of stability and acceptance.

As with the children at the centre of the stories in this part, it is not unusual for children to fear that difficulties or change have happened because of some deficiency in themselves. They may feel that they have done something wrong, or failed to do something right. For example, a child might believe that if she had taken better care of her mother, her mother would not have gone to hospital. Another child might worry that if he had not made so much noise, his father would not have left the family. Younger children especially can be very egocentric in their thinking. They have difficulty understanding events from the perspective of another, and therefore they attribute what has happened to some action of their own. I remember my little niece who visited her terminally ill grandfather in hospital. She had some chocolate buttons and he told her that this was just what he needed to get better. It was months later that she asked her mother if her grandfather had died because he didn't eat her chocolate buttons! This little girl was lucky – she was secure in her family and was therefore able to talk about her fears and worries and be supported with these. Without this sensitive support a child is left alone in confusion. This can lead to the experience of a range of emotional difficulties: increased anxiety, shame, anger or sadness. Often these difficulties are displayed through challenging behaviours, the language of communication when children cannot put it into words. The behaviour can end up being the focus of the adults as they struggle to provide containment, and the internal experience of the child becomes lost. Stories can help to remember and give voice to the internal world, leading to the child receiving the support he so desperately needs.

Stories can therefore be an important part of helping children understand transition, change and permanence. The examples in this part demonstrate how stories can be created metaphorically for the child using animals to represent the child and the child's family members. Similar stories have been written using toys or objects, depending upon the child's interest. The child's family experience is replicated using these characters. This allows the child to reflect upon this experience indirectly and thus to gain a coherent sense of what has happened to him. It provides hope that this is survivable and others can help him to feel more comfortable with this experience.

Similar stories can be written biographically or autobiographically, allowing the child a more direct experience of reflecting upon her circumstances and how others might help her with this.

Children can be active partners in this story creation, helping put the story together with the aid of pictures and props if that is helpful. For example, children might choose the pictures or props that best illustrate their family experience. They might help create the story, or they might illustrate the story with drawings or clip art. Alternatively, stories might be created through artwork or sand play to provide a more visual and experiential exploration of life story experience.

This life story work can occur within the family with the help of supportive parents or other family members. It might occur as part of social work support or it might be woven in to therapeutic interventions.

Part II
COPING IN FEAR AND WITHOUT TRUST

Story 4

Connor, the Superhero

Story type: Trauma; Therapeutic, with elements of Life story and Insight

Themes: The use of fantasy and superheroes; Trying to be strong; Staying in control; Anticipating rejection

Age range: 7–12 years

Family life is rarely uneventful, but even small changes within the family can increase the stress for children. Bigger changes can lead to more extreme strategies for coping. Children who have had several changes of family in their short lives can feel highly insecure. As we explored in the last story, it can be difficult for them to trust and settle into a permanent family, whether through step-parenting, adoption, foster or kinship care.

These children often experience a pervasive feeling of shame. The experience of shame is a normal part of toddler development, but when the child is not helped to manage this experience by a sensitive, attuned parent, they are left with a dysregulated experience of shame. This means that they are overwhelmed by the emotion, with no way of integrating or managing this. This leads to the development of a sense of self as not good enough. In other words, the experience of shame, feeling bad about self, becomes part of the sense of identity. The child feels like a bad person. The child develops a sense of self-hatred that leads to the anticipation of rejection. 'I'm not good enough; I don't deserve to be loved; they won't want me.' Love feels conditional: 'I will only be loved if I am good. I cannot be good all the time – therefore I will not be loved.' All this anxiety makes it difficult for them to respond to their parents in a straightforward way. These children cannot confidently seek comfort or security when they need it. Instead, they adopt controlling patterns of behaviour. These behaviours bring a fragile, short-term sense of security until the insecurity builds up again.

This also means that they do not have a secure base from which to go out into the world. School becomes very difficult as the children similarly do not trust or feel secure with the teachers and other educational staff. They become hypervigilant to signs of danger and rejection. Their focus becomes on this rather than learning. If relationships with adults are difficult, friendships with peers can be extremely uncomfortable. These children often elicit rejection from their peers as their behaviours can make them unpredictable and challenging. When they do interact with other children, their tendency to be bossy and controlling means that these interactions often don't go well.

These disorganized–controlling patterns of relating are well described in terms of Attachment Theory (e.g. in relation to children living in foster care or those who are adopted; see Golding 2008). Children develop strategies to feel some security in an unsafe world by interacting with others in highly controlling self-reliant or coercive patterns of behaviour. Whilst these behaviours might lead to some short-term sense of safety, unfortunately they are counter-productive in the long term. The responses of others to these controlling behaviours only serve to increase the insecurity the children are experiencing, and they will redouble their efforts to feel in control. The children are like hamsters in hamster wheels – the wheels move faster the longer they are running. They keep trying to run faster, but can't let others help them to get off.

At the root of much of the controlling behaviours that the children display is a lack of trust, leading to a need to be more self-reliant. Managing by themselves provides some security against the inevitable rejection that the children predict. This next story was inspired by a ten-year-old adopted boy who demonstrated his lack of trust through oppositional angry behaviour. He feared being sent away and tried to manage by himself. He did not trust in his parents' availability. Unfortunately, within the first year of being adopted, his father had been very ill, including a period of hospitalization. The boy learned that dependence was to be feared, and thus sought for premature independence. Trying to be independent whilst still needing dependence can be very frightening. Sometimes children will compensate for this fear through a fantasy life. They imagine being strong and invincible, in control in the most extreme of ways. This story was written using the fantasies the young boy shared with me. My aim was to help him have a context for these fantasies and to open up new possibilities for him.

Connor, the Superhero

Connor tensed his muscles, all of his body, ready for action. He quickly looked around – no sign of the enemy. Connor was not concerned; he could take on anyone and win. He was big and strong and courageous. He walked on down the cliff top road, glancing left and right. He was invincible, but it was best to know what he was going to meet. He could feel the energy flowing through his body; he needed to act soon or he would burst. The sun glinted on the sea in the distance and birds flew and dived over the cliff edge. Connor watched them, smiling to himself. He loved to fly with them, feeling the freedom of the air around him and the space beneath his feet. Not today though, today he was walking, the ground solid beneath him.

Then he heard it, screams coming from down the road. Quickly he ran to the source of the noise. He could see a big red bus; it had driven off the road and was leaning precariously on the cliff edge. Connor ran towards it and could see the scared faces of the people inside. No problem – Connor knew he could lift the bus, with his little finger if he needed to. Today he settled for his arms. He lifted the bus high above his head; the screams were louder now, the people inside unsure what was happening. Connor took a couple of steps and then gently put the bus back onto the road...

"Connor!"

The cross voice of his mother penetrated through the daydream Connor was enjoying. Guiltily he became aware that she was asking him to do something. He had no idea what she was asking.

"Come on Connor, how many times do I have to ask you?"

Connor looked at her, hoping for some clue as to what she wanted. He could feel the tension rising within him. He curled up his fists as anger rose within him.

"Right, I have had enough of this. I want you upstairs, teeth cleaned and down again in the next five minutes. I don't want to be late for school again."

With some relief, Connor moved towards the stairs, knowing now what he had to do.

"About time too; why don't you ever do what I ask the first time I ask?"

Connor heard the anger in his mother's voice and his own anger rose in return. He was never any good for her. Didn't she know he was a superhero, brave and strong, and courageous! But deep inside a small voice whispered: "No you're not. You are just a weak, little boy. They will send you away you know. They are not going to love you when you are so bad."

Connor exploded, fear and anger combining to give him the strength he had just been dreaming of. He flew at his mother; not thinking any more, he just needed to get rid of the fear and rage within him. Dimly he was aware of his father there too, of being picked up and put in his bedroom. He heard them talking as they walked away. He knew what they were saying. They were planning how to get rid of him. They would send him away this time for sure. Connor could think no more as his rage spent itself on his room. Finally he lay down amongst the chaos he had created. Emotionally drained, he fell asleep.

> Connor was walking down the road; the bus had resumed its journey. Still alert for danger, Connor carried on in the direction he had been travelling. He noticed the school bully coming towards him. Connor smiled as the boy glanced across and quickly walked the other way. No one would take him on. He was too strong for them all. He heard a car coming up behind him just as he was approaching a bend in the road. Suddenly Connor tensed up as he was aware of another car travelling fast towards them. Quickly Connor jumped between them, one hand stopping each car so that the crash was averted. He saw his father's face in one of the cars. He could save him...

"Connor, wake up. Here, I have a drink for you."

Blearily Connor was aware of his father next to him. He was confused. Surely his father had been in the car? How come he was here? Connor blinked as his bedroom came back into focus. The memory of what he had done came flooding back. Connor jumped back ready to fight again. His father's strong arms held him. His father lifted him onto his bed and sat down next to him. Connor did not look at him. He did not want to see his father's face, frightened of what he might see. His mother came too, and Connor relaxed slightly as she sat next to him and took him in her arms.

"Come on now, it's over. Have your drink."

"I don't want to go." Connor looked at his mother, fear in his eyes.

"You don't want to go to school? Is that what this is about?"

Connor grasped the straw they had offered him. He buried his deeper fear and agreed. "Yes, I don't want to go to school. Not today."

"Oh Connor, why didn't you just say, instead of getting so cross? We could talk about it. You have to go to school, but not today. Why don't you tell us what is worrying you? Are the other kids being mean again? Or are you worried that the teacher is still cross with you for breaking that window last week?"

Connor breathed a sigh of relief. He could talk about school. He wasn't being sent away. Not today. He leant in to his mother as his father crossed over to the window. He opened it wide, allowing some fresh air to enter the room. Connor looked across just in time to see his father jump back, astonishment in his eyes. Something swooped in through the open window!

Connor couldn't believe what he saw. It was like the boy he had dreamed about, big and strong and courageous.

"Hello Connor; hello Mum and Dad." The boy spoke with a deep confident voice. "I am here to help you."

"Are you a superhero?" asked Connor.

"Yes, I suppose I am. My name is Ronnoc, and I have come because you need help. I am big and strong and brave. I can help you figure this out. I know you are scared. I know you want to be brave and strong. I know you are frightened."

"I'm not frightened of anything," Connor protested. "I am brave and strong too."

Ronnoc smiled. "Of course you are, but you are also small and frightened. Oh wouldn't it be great to always be brave and strong? Then you wouldn't need anyone. Everyone would be safe and you wouldn't need to worry any more."

And then Ronnoc talked. He told the story of Connor's life. This was known to all of them, but the way Ronnoc talked about it made it seem different, clearer somehow.

Connor had never known his birth mother, but Ronnoc understood that there was still a hole inside of him because he had left her as soon as he was born. This was the beginning of his fear. Losing his birth mother so early had started a thread of fear. A thread that said that Connor was not good enough, that his parents got rid of him because he was bad.

Connor lived with a foster mother. He was only a baby. He did not understand that she was not his forever mother. Connor loved her but she was distant, never quite giving him the love he needed. It seemed to Connor that she got rid of him too. The hole inside of Connor grew bigger. The thread of fear grew stronger.

Connor was older now. He came to live with his parents. He had another mother and a father for the first time. He grew especially close to his dad. No dad had left him before, so it felt less complicated. These parents had adopted him, but Connor didn't understand this. He waited for this to end too. When would they send him away?

And then he thought it was happening. His father didn't come home. He did not know why, but the thread of fear was there, telling him what to believe. This was it. He wouldn't have a father any more. His mother tried to help him understand that his father was poorly. He would be home again, but not for a while. Connor didn't understand. He knew parents got rid of him. He believed his dad would get rid of him too. Connor felt all alone. He needed to be brave and strong. He wanted to need no one. He would be a superhero; only then could he stop the bad things happening.

Dad did come home, but Connor still tried to manage all by himself. He tried to be brave and strong. He grew older; he went to school. Always he would be tough; always he would be braver and stronger than everyone else. Then he would not need anyone. Then it would not matter if he was sent away. Connor buried this fear deep inside of him. He wrestled with his dad, shouted at his mum, and fought the children at school. He dreamt about being a superhero.

Connor and his mum and dad listened to Ronnoc. This was a story that was familiar to them, but new at the same time.

Connor's mum and dad told Connor, "We think we understand now. We didn't know that when you fought and when you dreamt you were trying to be brave and strong. We did not know how much you feared losing us. We did not understand that you thought we were going to send you away. How scary to live with this fear all the time. You are a superhero; you have been battling these fears all alone. That takes bravery and strength. We thought we could fill the hole inside you, but we think it has got covered up by the thread of fear and nothing is filling it up any more."

And Connor looked at Ronnoc and then at his mum and dad. "I am afraid but I try to pretend that I am not. I thought if I was brave and strong I could stop all the bad things happening. I am not a superhero, I am just a young boy, and I am frightened I am going to lose you."

Ronnoc and Connor's mum and dad looked at Connor and smiled. "You are a superhero," they said. "You may not be able to do magical deeds, but you are brave and strong. But you do not need to be a superhero alone. Together we can all be brave and strong. You can't believe that we won't send you away. We will believe for you. You can't believe that we will love you as you are, good and naughty. We will stay; we will love all the parts of you, the good, the brave, the strong and the naughty. You are a superhero to us, and one day you will know this too."

Connor looked at his mum and dad but he was not sure. He liked what they were saying, but the fear was still there. Ronnoc held his hand and this time he did not push the fear away. It was his fear, and, with his parents' help, he could live with it. He looked at Ronnoc. "Will you stay and help me too?" he asked.

"I have always been there," said Ronnoc, "you just didn't see me except in your dreams. I am your superhero and together we are brave and strong."

Story 5

Millie and Her Mother

Story type: Therapeutic; Insight

Themes: Fear and learning to trust; Longing, but resisting a mother's love; Mother's sadness; Building hope

Age range: 10 years and upwards, and adults

One of the most difficult of the controlling behaviours that children can display is a pattern of highly rejecting behaviours. This is often linked to a fear of being close or, more accurately, a fear of loss of closeness. In my experience it is the mother who is generally the focus of this rejection. The children continually push the mothers away with sometimes cruel and always rejecting behaviours. These behaviours are at their most extreme when the children are not getting what they want. Either being told 'no' or 'not yet' can provoke extreme behaviours; the child appears 'spoilt' but is actually expressing a sense of desperation – 'If I am not deserving of this, then I am not deserving of anything.' A mother once told me of the end to what had been a really lovely day with her daughter. It was a rare occasion when they had been out and all had gone well. The child had chosen some new clothes, where to go for lunch and an afternoon activity. Breathing a sigh of relief that there had been no rages or meltdowns to deal with, they returned home. Once home the child asked her mother to do something with her; the mother told her that she would have to wait whilst she finished what she was doing. The rejection was as desperate as it was unexpected. The child raged at her mother, screaming at her that she was not her real mother; she didn't want to live here any more; she was going to find her 'real' mummy and live with her.

These behaviours appear totally unreasonable and very hurtful, but they stem from very real fears – the child's beliefs that she is not good enough, that she is going to be rejected, are triggered by these very normal situations leading to behaviour that is extreme. Understanding this and living with it are two very different things, however. It is hard to stay patient and calm in the face of such rejecting behaviours. Parents are vulnerable to feelings of guilt, fear and depression as nothing they do seems to make a difference. They learn to distrust good times – lovely moments with the child – as they anticipate the rejection that so often follows.

This story was written with this situation in mind. It describes the fear and sadness that child and mother can experience within this pattern of behaviour.

Millie and Her Mother

A little girl called Millie stands at a cliff edge looking over a ravine. She gazes across at a mother. This is her mother, but it is difficult for Millie to believe this. She has had other mothers and has watched them go away. She does not want to trust this mother.

Her mother calls to her, but Millie tries not to listen. Her mother tells Millie that she will keep her safe. She will help her cross the ravine. She will build a bridge and she will hold her as she crosses.

Fear stands next to Millie. He tells her not to listen. "Do not trust this mother; stay with me. I will keep you safe instead."

Millie listens to Fear and shouts across at her mother. She tells her to go away; she does not want to be her daughter. Fear will keep her safe.

Fear smiles and encourages Millie on.

Millie's mother stands looking across at her daughter. She reaches out to her, using her strength to keep Millie safe. She builds a bridge ready for Millie to cross. She stays there waiting for her. But waiting is hard.

Sad stays with Mother, trying to support her. Sad is full of despair. She whispers in Mother's ear: "She will not love you, she will not come. Give up, turn away."

Millie's mother tries not to listen to Sad, but it is hard. Sometimes Sad persuades her and Millie's mother turns away. She sits, her back to the ravine, and lets Sad comfort her, but Sad's words are harsh.

"You are no good as Millie's mother; she will not come to you. Give up; stay with me instead."

Millie's mother blocks her ears. "I will not listen to you Sad. You are wrong. I am strong. I will help Millie cross the ravine. I will love her always."

Millie and Fear notice Millie's mother turning away.

"Look," says Fear. "See, she doesn't love you. She will not help you."

"But look," says Millie. "She is turning back towards me. She is there for me. I want her to hold me, to keep me safe. I will go to her."

Fear is angry. He shouts at Millie: "You listen to me. I know what's best. You stay here with me, don't go to her."

Millie is confused. She does not know what to do. Fear makes her feel angry.

"How do you know you will always love me?" she shouts to her mother. "Fear will always stay with me. It is safer to stay with Fear."

These are brave words, but inside, Millie's heart is breaking. Fear cannot love her as a mother can. She longs to be in her mother's arms, but her longing disturbs Fear.

"Turn away Millie. Come with me. I am stronger than your mother."

They stay like this for a long time. Sometimes Millie moves across the bridge a little way, and her mother's long arms are there to keep her safe, but always Fear calls her back. She retreats back to the cliff edge. Fear rejoices and his anger threatens to overwhelm Millie.

One day, as they are standing like this, mother and daughter either side of the cliff edge, a stranger comes along. She is out for a summer stroll. She notices the two of them and is curious. She comes over to see who they are.

Fear notices her. "Who are you?" he asks.

"I am Hope," she replies. "I am wondering about this little girl. She looks lost and lonely."

"She is fine," says Fear. "Leave her alone, I am taking care of her."

Hope looks at Fear. "It is not Millie who is lost and lonely is it? It is you."

"No," says Fear. "How dare you! I am fine. I have Millie."

Hope crosses the bridge. She looks at Millie's mother; Sad stands between them, protecting her from Hope.

"I am wondering about this mother," says Hope. "She looks full of despair."

"She is fine," says Sad, "leave her to me; I will help her."

Hope looks at Sad. "It is not Mother who is full of despair, is it? It is you."

Sad cries. "No, she says I am fine, I am here to help her."

Hope thinks hard and has an idea. "Come with me Sad. Trust me, I think I can help."

Sad looks at her; she is unsure. Hope smiles and Sad finds herself going with her. They cross the bridge together.

Hope takes Sad to Fear. "I think you two can help each other."

Hope waits with Millie whilst Sad and Fear talk together. They talk and talk. Sad talks about her despair, and how she is helping Mother. Fear talks about his anger, and how he is keeping Millie strong.

"How can your anger keep Millie strong?" says Sad.

"How can your despair help Mother?" says Fear.

As they talk, Sad starts to feel less despair and Fear starts to feel less angry. A friendship grows between them, and each feels less lonely.

"Go on," says Hope. "You have each other now."

"But what about Mother?" says Sad.

"What about Millie?" says Fear.

"I will help them, trust me. You two help each other."

As Fear and Sad leave, Millie's mother feels stronger. She walks out on to the bridge and calls to Millie.

"Go on," says Hope to Millie. "Go to her."

"How do I know?" says Millie. "How do I know she will always love me?"

"She will always love you," says Hope. "Trust me."

"But what about when she gets cross with me? Then she won't love me."

"Sometimes she will get cross with you," says Hope, "but she will still love you."

"But what about when she says no to me? Then she won't love me."

"Sometimes she will say no to you, but she will still love you."

"But what about when she doesn't do what I want? Then she won't love me."

"Sometimes she won't do what you want, but she will still love you."

Millie walks towards the bridge. Hope gently encourages her on. "Go to her; see, she is waiting for you. She will keep you safe."

Millie walks across the bridge and into her mother's arms. They walk away from the ravine together. They look back at Hope.

"Thank you," they say.

"I am here when you need me," says Hope. "You can trust me."

Story 6
In the Eye of the Storm

Story type: Therapeutic; Insight

Themes: Emotional avoidance; Developing self-reliance; Finding strength in feeling

Age range: 13–18 years

Growing up fearing others and with little trust that parents are available to meet emotional needs is very difficult. By their teens these young people will work very hard to avoid having needs that they might need support with. They do not admit to feeling worried, anxious or afraid. In this way they can persuade themselves that they can manage without relationships in their life. Although less socially skilled because of this, they believe that they are stronger. If they do not look for comfort in relationships, they will not be let down. No one can hurt them if they do not want relationships. Sometimes they concentrate intensely on their schoolwork, a safer focus than on the complicated world of friendships. They might love to read, burying themselves in books for hours of the day. Some of these young people like to invent fantasy worlds that they can exist within. The control over these worlds allows them to explore how to relate to others in ways that they would never do in the real world. I once met one highly intelligent girl living in foster care who had invented a highly complex world for herself. When not focusing on her schoolwork, she spent much of her time in this fantasy. She had imaginary friends, even a boyfriend, within this world. Although she did also have school friends who she would spend some time with, whenever these relationships became stressful, it felt safer to retreat back to this imaginary world.

Another foster girl I knew liked to use the Stargate universe for her fantasy life. This was a popular science fiction series that gave her lots of scope to explore relationships whilst she could remain firmly in control. She did not understand why I would want her to become more open to the real relationships around her. She only saw this as a route to pain and rejection. I wrote this story as a way of helping her to see my perspective about this, and why I thought real relationships were worth the risk.

In the Eye of the Storm

(This story first appeared in K.S. Golding (2008) *Nurturing Attachments: Supporting Children Who Are Fostered or Adopted.* London: Jessica Kingsley Publishers.)

Sam and Jack stepped through the Stargate into a world that they had not seen before. They looked around curiously, but found nothing remarkable. The sun shone brightly in the sky and the landscape was green and lush. They had been sent out on a reconnaissance mission to assess the possibility of sharing technology with the inhabitants. It was also a time for the two of them to spend some time together, time to come to terms with feelings for each other that they were unable to share or talk about.

They walked forward tentatively, but had not got more than 200 metres when a woman appeared as if from nowhere. She quickly walked towards them. From a distance she didn't look any different from the humans they had left behind on the other side of the Stargate, but as she got closer, they had a feeling that there was something different about her. Her eyes had little expression, it was hard to see what she was thinking, and her face was almost mask-like. Sam and Jack felt uneasy. They didn't really know what to expect. However, the introductions passed smoothly. The stranger, whose name was Trance, accepted their presence on the planet without fuss, and they were soon following her to a nearby city. Here they were greeted like minor celebrities and found little time to talk to each other as they were shown around the city.

In many ways the level of technology was not dissimilar to Earth except for one interesting aspect. The planet had a hostile climate for six months of the year, during winter, when the inhabitants all lived underground. A team of mechanics worked all year round, maintaining an environment that could sustain the population through the worst of the season. Trance was one of the mechanics. Jack paid particular interest to this. Here was a possibility for sharing technology that might be to Earth's advantage. He followed Trance around as she went about her duties. Jack admired her calm efficiency and ability to cope with minor crises without getting ruffled. She worked closely with a man called Brix, and the two appeared a competent and efficient team. Jack spent the next two weeks in the company of these two, which he enjoyed. He liked spending time with Sam, but it was always a strain. He had to work hard to keep his feelings hidden. The ironic thing was that he knew she was doing the same. They had agreed long ago that working in the same team meant that they shouldn't have a romantic relationship, but it was difficult to maintain this when working in such life-and-death situations. Jack envied Trance and Brix's easy relationship; they could clearly depend on each other, but there was no underlying tension.

At the end of the two weeks Sam and Jack went back through the Stargate to report their findings. They felt sad to be leaving the planet, as their stay here had been a welcome change from the usual danger and high drama. They eagerly looked forward to returning. They didn't have long to wait. General Hammond was excited by the possibility of technology exchange, and soon had a negotiation team ready.

As soon as Sam and Jack stepped through the Stargate again, they knew things had changed. The climate was very different. Storms were clearly brewing and there was a feeling of static in the air. Winter had arrived earlier than expected. Fearing a worsening in the climate at any moment, the team hurried to the nearby city. When they arrived the sense of panic was palpable. Sam and Jack didn't wait to be asked. They fell in with the rescuers, helping out where they could. As they took orders from the men coordinating the rescue, they gathered that the early arrival of winter had caught everyone off guard. The first field generator, which was meant to control the impact of storms, had overloaded. As it failed, the other generators had to cope with the force of the storm. Now each was failing in turn under the excessive load. If this increasing failure was not arrested, the storm would arrive in the city and they would all perish.

Sam and Jack worked alongside Trance and Brix for 18 hours. It looked as if they were winning. Parts of the town were now made safe and they were thinking about taking a break. Jack glanced over at Sam. Her hair was matted, and her face was covered in grime. Fleetingly Jack felt an ache of sadness that she could never be more than a friend. It was an ache that was suppressed with a speed that only comes from practice. He stepped back and fell in line with Trance. Brix and Sam followed closely behind. They had not gone far when there was a huge explosion behind them. They sprinted for the door as the blast from the explosion hurtled towards them. With relief, Jack threw himself through the door, Trance just behind him. Many hands reached out and grabbed them. In the confusion Jack could see no sign of Brix or Sam. A team of fire fighters worked furiously to contain the fires, but it was another 20 minutes before all was under control. During that time and despite his protestations, Jack found himself in the infirmary.

Jack put up with the medical examination with an impatience borne of worry and dread. Finally he was allowed to go. He looked around the infirmary for Sam, but could find no sign of her. He rushed back to the maintenance area. Scanning the mass of people, he finally spotted Trance calmly working at a control panel. Jack called to her, asking where Sam and Brix were. Trance looked at him coolly, and informed him that they had been trapped in the control room when the explosion occurred. It was unlikely that they had survived. Jack looked at her in horror, but Trance had returned to her task, unmoved by the news she had just imparted. Anger welled up in Jack. He grabbed Trance and wheeled her around.

"What are you doing?" he shouted. "We need to go and look for them."

Trance stared at him with her calm, impassive gaze. "We would be of no use; there are people working to make the room safe and then they will go in. It is imperative that we get this system going."

"Don't you care? How the hell can you be so calm?" Jack shouted. "Brix is in there."

"It is highly likely that Brix will not survive," replied Trance. "I can do nothing about this."

Jack's anger dissipated as his bewilderment increased. "How can you be so unfeeling? You have just lost your colleague and friend."

"A new colleague will be assigned to me."

"Don't you feel anything?" asked Jack.

"No, I am not programmed to feel. It is not necessary in my job."

Realization hit him like cold ice down his spine. She was an android. Now her difference from them made sense. "Are you all androids?" queried Jack.

"No, only half of the population is. There was such loss during the storms 50 years ago androids were necessary to ensure the survivors could rebuild."

Jack turned away. "I'm not so ready to give up on Sam. I'm going down there."

Twenty minutes later Jack was sitting wearily outside the door of the control room. Despite his best efforts, he had not been allowed through the door to look for Sam. He sat disconsolately looking at the floor when Trance came to him, a cup of tea in hand.

"I think you may require sustenance," she said, as she handed the tea to Jack. Jack cradled the cup in his hand as Trance sat down beside him. Jack looked at her. "I can't imagine what it is like not to feel anything in a situation like this."

"I think maybe I am in a good position," replied Trance. "Looking at you, feelings are very painful. Maybe I am better without them. If I don't feel, then I won't hurt."

At that moment the doors were finally opened and the rescue team entered the room where the explosion had occurred. Jack rushed past them scanning for Sam. It was difficult to see anything through the smoke and dust. Many dead bodies were carried out past him as he continued his hunt. There did not appear to be any survivors. Hope was dying within Jack but he refused to give up. They had been in tight spots before and had always managed to get out of them. He looked across to the side of the room and noticed an alcove blocked by fallen masonry. He walked over to it and peered through. He spotted Sam lying at the side, her arm flung over Brix. He could not see if she was breathing. He felt Trance come up behind him as he began moving the concrete out of the way. Trance pointed to the ceiling where a slab of concrete could fall at any moment. Urgently they manhandled the last beam away, and Jack pushed his way through. They had no time to assess Sam and Brix's condition. Jack pulled Sam clear as Trance lifted Brix out of the rubble.

They were back in the infirmary again, but this time Jack felt no resentment. He smiled at Sam as the nurse adjusted the bandage she had wound around her head.

"Not a pretty sight," Sam said weakly.

"It looks good from where I am sitting," laughed Jack.

Brix and Trance stood nearby. "Thank you Sam. It was your quick thinking that saved us," said Brix. "If we had carried on heading for the door we would have been caught in the main blast. Pulling us into the alcove protected us from the worst of it."

A week later and all was under control again. The storms had abated, at least for now, and some time for repairs had been welcomed. With relief, Sam and Jack headed towards the Stargate. Trance accompanied them. As they prepared to leave, Jack looked across and saw emotion clearly registering in Trance's face.

"I am feeling sad that you are going," she explained to Jack.

"Hey, I thought you were the girl who didn't feel anything?"

"I asked to be programmed to feel emotion. Observing you, I think I may function better with feelings. I could see the pain you were feeling, but also the strength that it gave you. Without those feelings I don't know that you would have been strong enough to rescue Sam."

"He always finds a way," smiled Sam.

As they neared the Stargate, Sam and Jack touched hands very briefly, and stepped through.

Notes about Part II

The stories in this part were all written to explore the fear and lack of trust that children can develop when they have experienced parents' lack of availability. The children come to believe that they are bad in some way, and thus to anticipate rejection or punishment. By being strong and invincible, going it alone or not having feelings, the child attempts to delay this anticipated loss of parents, and thus insecurity is replaced with a fragile security. This security is built on independence without the safety net of successful dependent relationships. This can quickly move to insecurity again occurs when the children experience parents withdrawing from them in some way.

Stories can be an indirect way of exploring these relationship patterns with children and their parents. Together they learn how to understand the child's fear and lack of trust and to experience the possibility of different, more trusting ways of being together. This is a less threatening way of reflecting on their experience than talking about it directly. In addition, because the character's deepest fears and worries are accepted within the story, the child gets a vicarious sense that their own experience might also be accepted. The child is left with new perspectives and the possibility of a different way of being.

When introducing the story to the child it is helpful to allow her to hear this in the way that she finds most comfortable. Some children sit quietly, perhaps cuddled up to a parent whilst they listen. Other children want to be more active, perhaps even acting out parts of the story. Sometimes the story or part of it is rejected as too difficult at the moment, or the child will listen, but only whilst hiding under a blanket.

The child who listened to the story of Connor struggled to listen to the part of the story that described his early experience, although he loved the other parts of the story. This story was used within his therapy sessions. He did not want to hear the story at home. In a later session he again enjoyed the first part of the story. As I continued to read the rest of the story he commented that this was his experience and he wanted to leave the room. I offered to stop, but he asked me to continue reading to his parents whilst he stood on the other side of the door. Following this, he asked his parents questions about his birth family. The story helped him to reflect upon and ultimately integrate some of his experience of being adopted, but he needed to do this in his way and at his pace.

Ultimately the stories are part of the process of building security for children. The children will show us the way they want to listen to the story; we can trust in the storytelling process, and gradually the fear will reduce and the children will be able to enter into more healthy relationships.

Part III
I WILL DO IT BY MYSELF

Story 7
Born to Care

Story type: Solution; Life story, with elements of Insight

Themes: Caregiving but not carereceiving; Coping with feelings of guilt; Developing self-reliance; Using self-harm

Age range: 13–18 years

Children who are controlling, aggressive and/or rejecting are very difficult to live with. Their behaviours are challenging, and parents frequently describe how on edge they feel, waiting for the next 'episode'. They feel like they are 'walking on eggshells'. These behaviours often stem from a need to be self-reliant, an effort not to signal their need and to seek comfort. Equally difficult are the children who are self-reliant in more withdrawn ways. These are the children who don't want to be noticed, who will not complain and who try not to draw attention to themselves. They smile, but this has no relationship to how they feel inside. They can be in pain but will not complain. For example, I have known parents who have discovered by accident that their children have large abscesses in their mouth, or even a broken arm, but the children have given no indication of the pain they are in. I remember one foster parent telling me of her foster son who had run into a lamppost; even whilst he was falling and before he hit the ground he was telling her that he was all right!

As I started to explore in the last story in Part II, if these children feel sad or worried or anxious, they try not to notice these feelings. They will also not seek comfort from others. They keep hidden the need for support and comfort whilst they express the need to explore, to help others or to manage by themselves. Exploration is the focus and is at the expense of attachment. These hidden and expressed needs are related to their expectations of others rather than how they feel internally. They are much better caregivers than carereceivers, often trying to take care of younger siblings or a struggling parent. For those children who move to foster care or alternative families, it is hard for them to give up these caregiving behaviours.

Whilst it is easy to miss the difficulties that these children are struggling with, this is done through a massive effort of emotional dissociation. The emotional experience is cut off from their awareness; the children don't just hide what they are feeling, they develop a way of not even experiencing this emotion. They notice only the superficial in their feelings. For example, I knew one boy who often got angry with a particular peer who could be quite horrible to him. The boy knew he felt angry, but could not see more deeply than this. He was astonished, as we worked together, to also discover how anxious this peer made him feel.

Emotions that are not attended to cannot be processed. Unmanageable, these emotions are driven from sight, but they do not go away. In fact, in being ignored, they can grow bigger. The first that parents and the child may know of the emotional struggle is when there is a huge emotional outburst. This appears unpredictable because the increasing stress that the child is experiencing has not been noticed or signalled. The 'meltdown' appears 'out of the blue'. These outbursts can also be quickly over as emotional control is achieved again, and the avoidance of feeling returns. This can leave others breathless, surprised and wondering if what they have just witnessed is actually real. If the child can return to 'normal' so quickly, could the emotion being displayed actually be genuine? It is very real, but the child has grown extremely skilled at hiding feelings away, and can quickly return to this state by cutting off from the emotional experience.

The next story was inspired by children who try to achieve this degree of self-reliance. It is the story of a young person who didn't signal his distress until the point at which he couldn't contain it any more. This teenager found it easier to be a caregiver than a carereceiver. This lack of balance between dependence and independence, however, can lead to major difficulties that eventually show themselves.

Born to Care

How hard it can be to ask for help. Sometimes there are just no words, especially when the words have not been taught to you from birth. Adults want to help, but it is hard to use this help when you have learned to go it alone. It is hard to know which adults to trust when adults seem to have let you down. It feels safer to find strength in independence. It feels safer to look after others than to be looked after. This is strength of a sort, but this hard-won strength can be its own weakness, and silent pain can be the hardest pain to bear. Jake understands this now, but this understanding took him a long time. This is Jake's story.

Jake is a young man who had a hard time growing up. The eldest of five, he silently watched his mum and dad fight and argue their way through a turbulent life. Sometimes they were together and sometimes apart, and when it was all too much, they took their own comfort in drugs and alcohol. And through all this the children kept on coming.

Jake, the first, was already a strain for his overwhelmed mum. She had grown up alone and unloved and did not know how to give love to her child. Jake learned quickly to expect little, and he rarely felt the warmth of a parent's embrace. When his sister was born he tried hard to give her what he himself had longed for. He felt good that he could take care of her, and he ensured that she was fed and warm. The third child, a brother this time, deserved nothing less. Jake felt himself 'born to care' as he gave the same attention to his brother as he had his sister. When Jake discovered his mother was pregnant for the fourth time, he felt his spirits sag. Could he do this again? He tried his best, and somehow he found the strength to embrace this brother too; his siblings grew up knowing that someone was interested in them, that someone cared for them.

As Jake entered high school another sister was born. Jake despaired, but reminded himself he was 'born to care' and set to the task of watching over her too. His schoolwork suffered, and potential friends passed him by. Teachers complained when homework wasn't done, and always his brothers and sisters were there, watching him with their silent brown eyes, imploring him not to turn his back. His mother too learned to depend upon Jake, especially as his dad left again, this time for good. She relied on Jake to get the children ready and off to school in the morning, and to collect them at the end of the school day. She relied on Jake to ensure she was up and dressed when the social worker called. She relied on Jake to hold their life together. Jake was strong, and he kept on going. He feared the help of other people. He did not tell the social worker. He did not tell the teacher. He feared what would happen if he did. Jake had no words to ask for help, only the strength to hold the family together.

When his eldest sister became ill, Jake tried to find the strength to help her to get better, but this was a task too many, and she was taken into hospital. She did recover, but in this recovery the mother's neglect became apparent. All the children were moved into foster care. Jake found himself in a placement with his eldest sister, but separated from the younger children.

Jake was strong, and he was 'born to care'. He thought he was strong enough to care for his mother and his siblings, but he wasn't. He felt guilty that he had not been strong enough. He ignored his guilt and tried to be stronger. He threw himself into caring for his sister. His foster parent tried to tell him it was okay, she could look after them both. Jake did not listen. He did not let the foster parent look after them. He tried to do it all by himself. His foster parent was kind. She offered love, and strong arms. Jake pushed them away. He had to be strong enough. He was 'born to care'.

Sometimes, though, in the dark hours of the night, Jake's guilt and weakness came to the surface. He thought of his younger brothers and sister. He mourned their loss. He suffered because he had not been strong enough; falling into restless sleep, he tossed and turned. The morning finally came and Jake got up, strong again. He pushed away his guilt, his weakness; he redoubled his efforts to take care of his sister. The foster parent looked at him with kind eyes. She asked him if he was okay. Jake almost gave in. His need to be taken care of grew a little inside of him, but he angrily pushed it away. He was fine, and anyway, he had no words to ask for help.

So time went by; winter turned to spring, and little by little, unlooked for, Jake's need to be cared for grew. Still he had no words to ask, but it became harder and harder to keep being strong. The more he cared for his sister, the more she needed him. Slowly and unnoticed, her need became a yoke around his neck; he was trapped in his strength, 'born to care' but not knowing how to be cared for.

Jake did not realize that his strength was his weakness. It took his words and gave him only action. All he could do was keep caring, and the more he cared, the less he asked to be cared for. Deep inside, his guilt and hurt grew bigger and stronger. It demanded to be heard. Jake tried not to listen. He tried to find his own words, but they had been lost so long ago he could not find them.

What do you do when you need to be cared for but you have no words?

What do you do when you need to be cared for but you have to be strong?

What do you do when you need to be cared for but you were 'born to care'?

Jake left the house and ran and ran. He ran until he was exhausted. He was not strong enough. Guilt overwhelmed him at last. He had failed. He had failed his mother, he had failed his younger brothers and sisters, and finally, he had failed the one sister he had left. Jake could take no more. He took a knife and pressed it into the soft flesh of his arm; slowly, carefully, he cut down his arm. He felt nothing as he watched the blood pool and then drip.

Finally Jake found the words. He picked up his mobile phone and called his foster home. "Help me," he said. "I need you to care."

This is Jake's story. It is a sad story. Jake wanted to share it with you. He knows now that he is not strong enough to care without being cared for. His strength was his weakness. In building this strength he lost the words he needed. He was 'born to care' but he was also born to be cared for. He didn't understand that, and so he did not use the care that was on offer to him. His actions had to speak louder when he did not have the words. He knows now that he could have found those words with the help of people around him. Jake carries a scar because he did not understand this. He hopes his story means that others will not make the mistakes that he did.

Slowly and carefully Jake is learning to let his foster mother care for him. Together they are building a vocabulary together. Jake now has words. He still cares about his sister, but together they are finally discovering the comfort of a parent's arms. Their birth mother is also being cared for. She, too, is getting stronger. The children will stay in foster care, but they all get together and visit their mum. She understands now that the children need to be cared for, and is glad that she has foster parents to help her. The younger children love to see Jake. He is strong. He is their big brother, but they like it that he now has words. He can ask to be cared for too.

Jake was 'born to care' but finally he has also learned to be cared for.

Story 8

The Boy with all the Knowledge of the World in His Head

Story type: Insight; Solution

Themes: Helping others; Developing self-reliance; Using emotional avoidance; Reliance on cognition

Age range: 8–14 years

Children can develop a whole range of defences in order to keep their emotions out of consciousness. They deny the negative feelings that they are trying to ignore and instead put on a cheerful exterior. Sometimes children enjoy being an entertainer, making everyone laugh and deflecting attention from their own internal experience. They are masters of distraction, denial and distancing from relationships. Parents will often report that the child is little trouble but that there is a problem in the relationship. It is hard to put their finger on what this is. Sometimes they feel as though they are not needed or that they are not important to the child. The child does not confide in them, but then they discover that she has been confiding in a relative stranger instead. When they suggest that the child might be feeling sad or worried, the child angrily denies this, the fear of being 'known' overriding the usual compliant, pleasing manner that she displays.

These children try and stay in control of their relationships through this premature self-reliance. This means that there are sides to relationships that they never learn to enjoy. These children have often missed out on the very early relationship experience that they need for healthy emotional development.

Infants and young children need to experience a relationship with a parent within which they feel safe. When they need comfort they are given it; when they are settled the parent helps them to explore the world. This describes an attachment relationship. In developing controlling styles of relating the children are not able to seek comfort and feel secure in the availability of the parent.

Additionally, children need a relationship within which they can experience themselves as having an influence on the other – an intersubjective relationship. A child and parent interact in synchrony, with the parent responding to the child and the child responding to the parent. A child delights in the responses they can elicit, and gains a deep sense of being known and understood. When children lack these early intersubjective relationships, they never learn the satisfaction of a relationship within which each mutually influences the other. They become bossy and controlling, managing the other person without allowing the other to influence them.

The lack of this healthy relationship experience early in life, and the subsequent development of controlling behaviours, influences the way the child relates to others. This can lead to difficulties with peers as he matures and moves out into the world. Other children can find him rather too adult, bossy and controlling. This can leave the child feeling isolated, or with friendships that are shallow and impermanent.

The next two stories are written for young people who have learned these avoidant styles of relating to others, revealed as extreme self-reliance and avoidance of emotion.

The first story was inspired by a child who found such relationships difficult – a charming, delightful ten-year-old who appeared older than his years. He liked to be in control, revealing little of himself and resisting attempts to connect with his internal emotional experience. He liked to be clever and entertaining. He hated feeling sad, worried or anxious. He used his intellect to keep his emotion at bay. Resisting negative emotion in himself, he dealt poorly with conflict or emotional distress in others.

The Boy with all the Knowledge of the World in His Head

(This story first appeared in K.S. Golding and D.A. Hughes (2012) *Creating Loving Attachments: Parenting with PACE to Nurture Confidence and Security in the Troubled Child*. London: Jessica Kingsley Publishers.)

Once upon a time there was a boy; his name was David and he was very special. He was very special because he remembered everything he was ever told. This made him very clever. As time went by he heard more and more and he stored more and more knowledge in his head. Soon he had all the knowledge of the world in his head.

Now, David was a kind boy, and he liked to help people. He liked to help his friends with their problems. Sometimes he helped them with their homework and sometimes he helped them with their hobbies. David enjoyed helping his friends. He enjoyed sorting out their problems and seeing how happy this made them.

David also liked to help his sister, but this was a little trickier. Sometimes she let him help her, but other times she didn't like it. She wanted to be clever too, and she didn't like to think that David could do things that she couldn't. She tried very hard to do things on her own and got very cross when David tried to help. Sometimes David got cross back, because he wanted to help her and he was upset that she wouldn't let him.

David also liked to help his mum and dad. They were pleased when he helped them, but sometimes they wanted to help David in return. This was a problem. David knew he had all this knowledge in his head, but they didn't understand this. They thought that David needed help with all sorts of things that he didn't need help with. Sometimes David got cross with them. They would try and talk to him, but David found it very difficult to explain that he didn't need help because he had all the knowledge of the world in his head.

One day David was at school when his friend, Simon, needed some help. Knowing that David was very clever at sorting out problems, he brought it to David. Now this problem was a very big one, and David went through all the knowledge in his head so that he could help his friend. He searched and searched for an answer, but despite all this knowledge, he couldn't find one. This made David very anxious. This was difficult. He didn't like feeling anxious. Feeling anxious made him feel strange. He tried very hard not to feel anxious. So when Simon kept asking him for an answer, David could feel the anxiety building up. He did not like this at all and he got very angry with Simon. He shouted at him and Simon ran away.

Now David felt sad as well. Feeling sad was as bad as feeling anxious. If you feel sad, all the knowledge in your head can't help you. David worked very hard not to feel sad. He wanted Simon to come back, but he couldn't explain this to him. Instead, he turned his back, and thought to himself that it was Simon's fault. Simon should not have a problem that all the knowledge of the world could not solve.

David was feeling very hot and bothered after school that day. He went home and was very cross with his mum. He would not have his snack and he would not play nicely with the other children. That night he had a judo lesson. Now David liked his judo class. He liked to feel in control of all the moves, and was working hard for his next belt. Tonight, however, he did not feel like going. He was trying very hard not to feel anxious or sad, and he was feeling tired. David's mum was very clever. She could see that David was struggling with something big, and she thought that going to his judo class might help. She encouraged him to go, and even gave him a lift down to the hall.

David did feel better doing the judo moves. He focused very hard and he found that he wasn't feeling so cross and bothered. During the break the judo teacher came up to talk to David. He had noticed how focused David was and guessed that something was troubling him. David was feeling a bit more relaxed now, and he found himself telling his teacher about the big problem that he could not solve, and his friend running away from him. He told him how cross he was when this made him sad and anxious. He thought that the teacher might laugh at him when he told him all this, but he didn't. He looked very thoughtful for a while, and then said that sometimes problems are bigger than all the knowledge of the world. Sometimes problems don't have easy answers, and you just need to be there for a friend.

David found tears in his eyes; he hurriedly fought them back so that they didn't show. How could he be there for his friend when he didn't have an answer? How could he be there when it made him feel anxious or sad? David's teacher helped him to see that, although he was very clever, he wouldn't always have the answers. Sometimes he might need someone to help him. David thought about his mum and dad. They were sometimes sad, and dad was very anxious when Uncle Bill was poorly. Maybe his mum and dad could help him when he felt sad and anxious. Then he would be able to help his friend.

That night David had a long talk with Mum and Dad. He told them about his friend. They told him how sad they were thinking about him trying to deal with this all alone. They knew his life had been hard, and sometimes it felt like his parents were no help at all. David felt tears prickling the back of his eyes. For the first time in his whole life he did not fight them but let them fall. Mum hugged him tight, and even had a few tears herself. David suddenly felt safe and warm and cosy. He snuggled in tighter, enjoying the feeling that he did not have to solve problems all by himself. David discovered that tears were not all bad, and being comforted by your mum and dad was close to being the best feeling in the world. The boy with all the knowledge of the world in his head had learned something brand new.

David discovered that there were more ways than one of being clever. He also learned that having feelings was not a weakness; feeling sad and anxious helped you notice when you needed some support from others. Mum and Dad understood about some things even better than him, and they could be there for him, to comfort and support him and even to help him when there were no answers. David was glad that he wasn't all alone, that he had Mum and Dad and his judo teacher to help him.

The next day at school David found his friend, Simon. He told him he was sorry that he had been angry with him, and explained that he didn't have an answer to his problem but he would try and be there for him. He told him that he wasn't good at feeling sad or anxious, but that he was working on it. Simon gave him a big smile and said: "It looks like we both have big problems; maybe we can help each other." David smiled back; even with all the knowledge of the world in his head he still needed some help from other people. David was very clever, but sometimes that just wasn't enough.

Story 9

The Mermaid's Song

Story type: Insight; Solution

Themes: Adopting false positive affect; Experiencing sadness and pain; Developing self-reliance; Coping with the fear of rejection

Age range: 7–12 years

Some children have had the experience, from early in life, of being punished for displays of negative emotion. Whether through a parent shouting or hurting them, or because a parent actively withdraws whenever such emotion is revealed, these children learn to stop displaying the negative emotion. This emotional inhibition can even be seen in infants. In the more extreme parenting environments this is not enough to help the children to feel safe. As they grow older they adopt even more extreme ways of avoiding such punishment. Now they don't just inhibit the expression of negative emotion; they learn to cover their experience by putting on a display of positive emotion (often called false positive affect). They appear smiling and happy, but this has little relationship to what they are experiencing internally.

Whether within their families or at school, these children are often seen as 'no trouble'. Their hidden needs for comfort and security are so well hidden that others do not even suspect that these needs are there. They can be helpful and kind, they like to take care of others and they always appear happy and cheerful. Helping these children to display negative feelings and to take comfort for themselves, to allow themselves to be cared for, is the challenge that the parents take on when they wish to help children who have become masters at hiding what they are experiencing.

This story was written for families experiencing children with false positive affect. It is a story that reveals the strength of the children but also their frailty.

The Mermaid's Song

Long ago and in a sea far away there lived a young mermaid. She was called Merisa. She was a graceful mermaid with dark hair and a sleek green and blue tail. She loved riding the waves as they crashed towards the shore, although of course, like all mermaids, she was careful not to be seen by the humans on the beach.

All the other merchildren thought Merisa to be the happiest of mermaids:

She smiled and she laughed as she played with her friends.

She smiled and she laughed as she kept the sea bed tidy.

She smiled and she laughed as she attended to her lessons.

But Merisa's song tells another story. Did you know that all mermaids have a song telling the story of their life? If you listen hard to Merisa's song you will hear a sad story. Merisa may smile and laugh, but deep inside her there is sadness and pain.

My story is sad for all who will hear,

Born into a world that is full of fear,

No mother's arms keeping me safe from harm,

No mother's voice helping me to feel calm,

Just arguments and fighting all around,

Lonely and longing, wishing to be found.

Little Merisa learned to live in this world. She grew strong and tough. She learned to need no one as she took care of herself.

Having no one to rely on she learned to rely on herself.

Having no one to wipe away her tears she learned not to cry.

Having no one to soothe her fears she learned to be brave.

All the other merchildren admired Merisa. She always knew what to do. If she scraped her tail as she was swimming, she did not cry. She shook her tail and got on with her swimming. She found her own food, and brushed her own hair. It seemed that there was nothing that Merisa could not do. She even took care of the younger merchildren when they were hurt or sad.

There was one thing that Merisa could not do, though, but she did not think it mattered. I wonder if you can guess what it is?

She could not allow others to care for her. She did not want to feel close to anyone.

I am stronger now I need you no more,

I swim in the water and reach the shore,

Sad or happy only smiles you will see,

Caring for myself, I strive to be free,

Closeness I lack, but without it I'll live,

I'll take nothing back, it is safer to give.

So Merisa learned to manage on her own, but she was noticed. A merman and merlady saw her. They saw her smiling and looking happy. They saw how she looked after the others. And they watched as no one took care of her. They felt sad for this young mermaid who, for all her smiles, looked so alone. They felt a longing in their heart and wanted to take care of Merisa. They called to her:

Come and live with us and we will hold and cherish you.

Come and live with us and we will give you all our love.

Come and live with us and we will support you as you grow.

So Merisa did go to live with this new mermother and merfather. She grew in height and in spirit. But old habits die hard. Merisa knew how to laugh and to smile, and she enjoyed sharing fun times in this new family. When she felt sad or worried, however, she hid this away. She did not want her mermother and merfather to leave her, so she kept hard things to herself. If she was in pain she told no one; if she felt ill she managed by herself. When things needed doing she quietly did them.

I live with you now, new family of mine,

I strive to be good, you'll not hear me whine,

Loving arms you have, I'm glad to receive,

Living here with you I hope not to leave,

And just to be sure I'll give but not take,

I'll look after myself, a fuss I won't make.

Now one day, a few months after joining her family, Merisa was out helping some of the younger mermaids build a garden on the sea bed. It was nearly time for tea, and not wanting to be late, Merisa was rushing to finish. She was just moving one of the larger rocks into place when she slipped and dropped it. The rock landed on her arm. With a great effort Merisa managed to get her arm free, and feeling a little sick she returned home. Merisa was quiet during tea, and could not eat for the throbbing in her arm. Mermother asked if she was all right. Merisa smiled and said she was a little tired. She went to bed early. All night long she lay awake trying not to cry out with the pain in her arm. The next morning she got up and tried to act normally, but when mermother gave her a hug she could not hide the wince of pain. When mermother looked, she saw Merisa's arm was swollen and blue. "Why didn't you tell me?" she asked as she called the merdoctor. The merdoctor nodded gravely. "I should have been called sooner," he said, as he attended to the arm. Merisa did not know what to say. "Will you leave me now?" she whispered.

Mermother and merfather held Merisa tight and whispered back. Can you guess what they said?

They told Merisa: "No, we will not leave. We are your family forever now."

Merisa's mermother and merfather knew that all merchildren need someone they can depend on, someone to help when they are hurt, to hug them when they are sad, to support them when they get things wrong. They understood that Merisa did not know this. They needed to teach her that they would always be there for her, even when she wasn't laughing and smiling.

Slowly and quietly they moved close to their merdaughter,

Slowly and quietly they took care of her even when she didn't ask,

Slowly and quietly they taught Merisa to ask when she needed help.

Merisa was still afraid at times. If she needed them, she still feared they would be gone. But little by little she grew in trust. The mermother and merfather opened their arms and the young mermaid could be held at last. The last verse of Merisa's song was created by them all.

Come here young mermaid, let me hold you tight,

Dare I come close? Are you sure it is right?

Yes it is right, in our arms you belong,

But trusting your care, will I still be strong?

Let us care, together real strength is made,

I'll relax in your arms, I grow less afraid.

And so Merisa grew up safe with her family. She learned that she could be sad as well as happy. She still smiled and laughed, but when she needed to cry, their loving arms were there to hold her. Merisa grew even stronger as she learned to be loved and taken care of.

Notes about Part III

The stories within this part were all written for children who have adopted controlling behaviours in order to attain a degree of self-reliance and independence from the adults caring for them. These are children who have learned to fear dependence early in their life. When a child experiences their dependency needs as overwhelming their parent, they feel insecure and so will try to suppress these needs. By developing some ability to be self-reliant and independent they experience their parent as less overwhelmed and so feel a little more secure. A consequence is, however, that they do not learn how to let others support their emotional needs; premature independence learned without the experience of successful dependence can lead to later relationship difficulties. The biggest cost to this self-reliant style of relating to others is that the children are not able to seek support from others when this would be helpful for them. All the stories in this part provide a degree of insight into this way of being with others.

The challenge when parenting or working therapeutically with children with this level of self-reliance and avoidance of emotional experience is that the children and young people themselves have already learned to do without intimate relationships and emotional connection.

In Part II I explored stories for children who did not trust adults to take care of them and so tried to become independent. The work with these children is to build the trust that they need so that they can become comfortable in dependence and emotional connection.

In this part the focus is more on children who have learned to manage without trusting relationships, and feel much safer as a consequence. They now do not want to start to form a relationship with a parent or a therapist. I worked with one teenager, for example, who told me that now she had learned to manage without close relationships she did not want to learn another way of being. 'Why,' she asked me, 'would I want to be open to relationships when I have spent so long learning not to need them?' These children can react very strongly to the experience of emotional connection, someone understanding the fears and worries buried deeply within them. They become angry, rejecting and more controlling to ensure that this emotional connection is not deepened. More than any others these children can benefit from the indirect connections that they can experience from metaphorical stories, or biographical stories of other young people with similar experiences. These stories can increase their understanding about why they feel more comfortable in self-reliance and the strengths that this can bring whilst also opening their eyes to the down-side of these strengths.

Helping the children to reflect 'at a distance' by talking in metaphors and using stories can be a starting point for developing a relationship. The children can safely explore their reliance on disconnection and what might be gained through connection – small but important steps towards exploring relationships at a more intimate level.

Additionally, stories can be written down and can thus be a helpful way of connecting with a child who cannot yet tolerate being in a therapy room or talking face-to-face with a therapist. A conversation through letters and stories might be all that they can cope with. Offering this indirect support conveys the message that the practitioner is interested in them whilst accepting the child's need to keep them at arm's length. Instead of blaming the child for resisting or not engaging in therapy, a stance that tends to close the door on providing help to the child, the responsibility is on the practitioner to find a way of supporting the child that is tolerable for her.

Part IV
KEEP NOTICING ME

Story 10

Melinda and the Golden Balloon

Story type: Therapeutic; Insight

Themes: Fears of abandonment; Developing attention-needing behaviours; Managing strong feelings

Age range: 7–12 years

Whilst some children's early experiences lead them to prefer not to be noticed and to be reluctant to engage deeply in relationships, other children have a different experience.

When children experience early caregiving as highly unpredictable and inconsistent, they are confused. They experience no reliable predictors for knowing that their parents are available and will meet their needs. Sometimes their parents appear to be noticing them and will offer them comfort and care, whether or not they need it at that time. At other times these same parents appear impatient or rejecting, experiencing the child as a nuisance. It can feel highly unsafe when children cannot discover any connection between their own internal experience and the responses of the parent. In this highly unpredictable world the children learn to be noticed at all costs. If parents are attending to them, they do not need to worry about their availability. They learn highly coercive ways of relating to parents and others that ensures some predictability in an unpredictable world. These are also controlling behaviours, but they draw people in to attending to them rather than keeping people at a distance. Unlike the children who inhibit their emotional experience, these children act out their emotional experience through extreme attention-needing behaviours.

When these children are being parented by parents who are more sensitively attuned to their needs, the children with this earlier experience do not understand or trust in this predictability. They continue to feel anxious and insecure and respond to this anxiety through displays of attention-needing behaviours. These behaviours are very intense and can be emotionally overwhelming for the parents trying to care for them. The sensitive parents try to meet the needs being signalled, but none of their attempts to soothe or reassure the child work. The child remains on high alert, ready to ward off unavailability by a constant thirst for attention. Eventually the parent withdraws from this onslaught of need, if only temporarily to catch their breath and restore their own emotional tanks. This withdrawal, however, is evidence to the child that nothing has changed; they cannot relax and trust in the availability of the parent. It can be lost at any time. The child's expectations of unpredictability and intermittent availability have been met, and their need to remain attention-needing is confirmed. Hidden needs to use the parent as a secure base from which to learn independence remain firmly hidden as the child expresses over and over 'notice me, notice me, notice me'. This is not related to how they feel internally, but stems from their expectation and fear that, once unnoticed, they will not be noticed again. Attachment is the focus, and it is at the expense of exploration.

The following story was written with these children in mind. This is a story that explores the unconscious drive to be noticed that some children display and the impact it can have on others. Rather than ignore these attention-needing displays, sometimes novel solutions are needed to help the child believe in the availability of the parent, and to help them to relax their vigilance and believe that a parent's attention will be there when needed.

Melinda and the Golden Balloon

Once upon a time and in a land far away there existed a golden balloon, as bright as the sun and as light as the air. This was no ordinary balloon – he had been enchanted some time before. Enchanted and then abandoned by a magician who was as clever as he was cruel. The balloon now lay in a quiet corner of the land, deflated and forgotten.

The balloon lay there thinking about all that he was missing and a longing grew in his heart – yes, an enchanted balloon has a mind to think and a heart to feel, just like any human. He longed for the magician to return and to inflate him, so once again he could float in the air instead of lying forgotten on the ground.

Now it happened one day that Melinda, a poor girl from the local village, was passing by. She had been out looking for work, and was returning home empty handed and with her head downcast, as she feared another hungry evening. She walked along thinking of little else but her empty cupboards when out of the corner of her eye she saw a glint of gold, as bright as the sun. Intrigued, she paused to look and found the balloon. Hesitating just a little, she bent down and picked him up.

"Well, you won't feed me or my family, but you are such a beautiful colour. I will take you home. Maybe you will give us some amusement so that we forget the hunger in our stomachs."

Much to her surprise, the balloon answered her.

"I would like that very much. I have been alone for such a long time. Please take me and maybe I can take your mind off your hunger. I will do my best to shine golden and bright for you."

And so the balloon and Melinda returned home together.

This began a happier time for the balloon. Melinda inflated him and they spent many an hour together. It was indeed as if the sunshine itself had come into Melinda's life, and the balloon felt loved and wanted for the first time. He also brought them luck because people loved the golden balloon and so were happy to give Melinda work. The family were no longer hungry.

The balloon and Melinda enjoyed being together, but the balloon could not be completely happy. Being able to think and feel meant that he was able to remember the past and worry about the future. He remembered those lonely years and fear entered his heart – fear of being abandoned again, being left forgotten and deflated in some bleak corner of the world. This fear ate away at the balloon. He enjoyed being loved and cared for, but what if this didn't last? What if Melinda tired of him and let him go? Could being a golden balloon be enough for her, or would she find other amusements, other friends, leaving him forgotten again?

As time went on this fear did not lessen – the balloon tried in lots of ways to make sure Melinda kept noticing him. He made himself bigger and brighter; he made lots of noise; he insisted that Melinda kept him inflated. He feared that if ever he deflated that would be it, he would be forgotten entirely. His fear got so bad that Melinda could go nowhere without him. She had to hold him all the time, hold him tight so that no air could escape.

Melinda tried to reassure the balloon. She told him she would never forget him. If he deflated she would always reinflate him again, but the balloon was not reassured. Some days the fear would get so big that the balloon worried he would burst. Then he got cross and angry with Melinda. This made Melinda cross too, and she would hand the balloon to someone else for a while whilst she calmed down, and of course this made the balloon anxious all over again. Then the balloon felt like the naughtiest balloon in the world. He believed that one day Melinda would realize how bad he was and would deflate him for good. He would be forgotten forever.

This was hard for the balloon, and it was hard for Melinda. Whatever they did, the balloon's fear did not reduce. Melinda began to feel very tired with the effort of noticing the balloon all the time. She could never relax and just enjoy being with him. The balloon too was working so hard to make sure that Melinda kept hold of him that he could not relax. He needed to be taken care of, but he could not enjoy it.

And so it would have gone on until both were worn out with trying so hard, but luckily Melinda had a friend, Owain, who was very wise. He could see how hard it was for Melinda to keep on looking after the balloon, but also that she did not want to give up on him. She loved the balloon, but it was so tiring holding on to him all day.

Owain thought very hard about how he could help his friend. The three of them would go out on walks, and the balloon looked his brightest and most golden at these times. It was as if the sun came with them as they walked. Owain talked to them both about how hard it was being a balloon that had been abandoned and how hard it was for Melinda to reassure the balloon that she would not abandon him too. As they talked, both the balloon and Melinda relaxed a bit; in fact, the balloon even managed when Owain held him for a while. As long as he could see Melinda, he enjoyed being held by someone else.

Then Owain had an idea. He went into his workshop and he made a necklace. This was a very special necklace made in two parts. Owain put into one part of the necklace all the brightness and golden colour of the balloon and in the other part he put all the love and kindness of Melinda. He then placed one part of the necklace around Melinda's neck. It shone golden and bright, reminding Melinda always of the balloon she loved. The other part was tied around the neck of the balloon. Now the balloon could not deflate and he would always have Melinda's love and kindness with him.

And so the balloon learned that he could spend time apart from Melinda and that he was never forgotten. He had part of Melinda always with him to remind him when the worries came again. He also knew that, wherever Melinda was, she had some of his golden brightness with her. She would not forget him.

Now Melinda could relax and enjoy being with the balloon again. She knew if she needed to leave him for a while he would be all right. He would know that he wasn't forgotten. The balloon could also relax and enjoy being cared for. He even came to enjoy times apart from Melinda, knowing that he would not deflate and be forgotten.

And all those who saw Melinda thought that she was the luckiest girl alive, for she always had sunshine in her life.

Story 11

The Clockmakers and the Cuckoo Clock

Story type: Therapeutic; Insight

Themes: Developing attention-needing behaviours; Being noticed through chatter; Acceptance; Need for predictability

Age range: 8–14 years

Attention-needing behaviours are very draining, both for the child and parents.

The child is tired from working so hard to be noticed. She cannot relax her guard for a moment; she must always remain vigilant to possible signs that the parents are not noticing her. This signals unavailability, and the fears of abandonment rise to the surface – fears of being forgotten entirely. The child fears that she could literally disappear from her parents' minds. This is a profound fear, much more than the fear of disapproval. In disapproval we are being thought about. Negative attention is so much better than no attention. The attention-needing child is working to continue to exist in the minds of the parents.

The parents are working hard to try and remain sensitive towards the child, available to meet all the needs being signalled so remorselessly; they are also juggling this with lots of other demands upon them, including making sure other children are not left out. Holding on to your patience in the face of multiple demands puts a large emotional strain on the parents.

Trying to tackle these behaviours head on rarely works – ignore attention-needing behaviours at your peril. The need grows bigger the less attention it is given. Similarly, behavioural management strategies, whether with rewards for independence or sanctions for neediness, just miss the point. They reinforce a sense of love as conditional – behave in this way and only then will I approve of you. These children are highly insecure; they do not fear disapproval, but that they are forgettable and unloveable, and that they will be abandoned one day. They need unconditional relationships – 'no matter what' rather than 'only if'. Predictability and acceptance of their insecurity is the path towards increased security. It is a long road and a hard one, but if parents can hang on in there, it will be worth it. After all, the starting point is a good one. The children want a relationship with them, but it is hard for them to feel secure within this relationship. In many ways this is easier than parenting a child who has decided his parents are not for him. With the attention-needing child the parent is half-way there already. In fact, if the relationship-resistant child is to find security within the relationship with the parent, he is very likely to go through the same attention-needing stage as the child who wants a relationship from the start. This is a road that needs to be travelled to help children who are insecure within families become secure.

Self-care is important to remain emotionally available. Parents will run out of patience, and that is all right. Parents will need time for themselves – respite breaks – and these are deserved; parents will need supportive friends and family, so that they are not alone. If parents can look after themselves in order to look after the child, the child will feel looked after indeed.

One of the most difficult of attention-needing behaviours for many parents is the constant chatter from the children. Not for nothing are these behaviours often called 'in your face'. The children have to fill every moment with talk, asking questions, often the same questions endlessly, and telling stories, demanding to know what is happening. They question, they ask, they demand, but rarely do they wait for an answer. It is actually attention, not answers, that they are looking for. The need to maintain the verbal link with the parent is constant. This gets even more heightened when the parent has their attention elsewhere. Trying to talk on the phone, or chatting to visitors, become insurmountable challenges as the child physically inserts herself between parent and the competitor for the attention.

This next story is written with these children in mind. It was inspired by a number of parents I have met, and their stories of their attention-needing children.

The Clockmakers and the Cuckoo Clock

There was once a clockmaker, the finest in the land. He had learned the craft from his own father and no one could surpass him in his craftsmanship. However, the Clockmaker was growing older and his eyesight was failing. He knew he would not be able to continue making fine clocks for much longer. He talked with his wife, and they agreed that once he finished his latest commissions he would finally retire and have the rest he deserved after so many years of clockmaking. Having no children of his own, his workshop would pass to his Niece. She had learned what she could of clockmaking from her Uncle, and was now away in a distant land, expanding her skill.

The Clockmaker was slower than he used to be, but at last he had fulfilled his obligations. All the clocks were made and dispatched to the right people. He just had one clock left, a small cuckoo clock. He had been working on this clock in his spare time as a gift for his Niece. He had laboured over the making of this clock, pouring his love and attention into it, and it was nearly finished. He had used the finest wood and had included the most delicate of carving on its exterior. The little cuckoo itself might be said to be his finest craftsmanship of all. It only needed its mechanism and the cuckoo would be given its voice; but alas, when the Clockmaker looked in his drawers, he found that he had no more springs left. He was old and tired; he no longer had the energy to travel to the Springmaker. He left a note for his Niece, explaining that the clock was nearly finished, and letting her know what she needed to do to complete it. With a last look at his workshop, he turned the key in the door and left the key where his Niece would find it. His long career as a clockmaker had come to an end.

It was a number of months before the Niece travelled back and took up ownership of the workshop. By that time a number of people wanted clocks made. They were growing impatient; they were concerned that she may not be as good as her Uncle; they were wondering about going to a new clockmaker. The Niece could waste no time. She needed to make the clocks and prove herself as good a clockmaker as her Uncle. She smiled when she saw the cuckoo clock, but for the time being had to leave it to one side. Business must come first.

Well, the Niece did prove herself an able clockmaker, every bit as good as her Uncle, and her business soon thrived. She was kept very busy as the orders kept coming in. Every so often she noticed the cuckoo clock. She would talk lovingly to it, promising to finish it soon, but it was hard to find the time, such was the pressure of work.

And so it might have continued but for a small chance one day; as the Niece was hunting in her drawers for some parts she needed, she found one of the drawers was jammed. She worked at it until it was freed, and discovered that a spring had stopped it opening, the very spring that was needed for the cuckoo clock. This spurred her on. With great care she finally finished the cuckoo clock and hung it proudly in her workshop. The cuckoo found its voice and proudly sung the hours. The Niece spoke to the cuckoo, admiring his colours and admiring his voice, feeling glad that he was there to keep her company whilst she worked.

The cuckoo loved this attention. He had felt very lonely, waiting for the clock to be finished. He had waited unnoticed for so long, powerless to do anything to get the attention he needed. But now he had a voice and the Niece loved him at last. The cuckoo was happy, but deep inside he had a gnawing anxiety. He did not want to be abandoned again. He did not want to feel lost and lonely in the clock. He liked being out, he liked having a voice. He feared that the Niece would tire of him. And so he used his voice, again and again. He chimed the hours, the quarters, the half hour, making sure she remembered him. The Niece smiled at this. The cuckoo's song marked the passing of the day; it comforted her as she worked. But still the cuckoo did not feel safe. A quarter of an hour was a long time to wait for reassurance that he wasn't forgotten. And so he started to sing in between. He sung every five minutes, and the gentle cuckoo took on a plaintive note: 'Notice me, notice me, notice me,' it said.

The Niece was concerned. She took down the clock and tried to adjust the mechanism, but whatever she did, the cuckoo kept on singing. The Niece did not know what to do. She spoke to the cuckoo, gently at first, but then with increasing frustration. She warned him that he could spoil her trade; people would not want clocks made by a clockmaker who could not get her own clock right. The cuckoo, hearing this, just became more anxious. He wanted to stop his endless song; he wanted to please her, but he could not stop. He had to be sure she did not forget him. He had to keep up his song. He most feared when customers dropped by the shop. She seemed lost to him then. He sang louder and even more frequently whilst they were there. Soon there were less customers coming to the shop. The Niece did not know what to do. The clock was important to her but so was her trade. She warned the cuckoo that if he could not be quiet, she would have to remove the spring again.

And so her threat might have come to pass except, just as she was feeling most desperate, there turned up at her workshop a Wise Woman seeking a clock of her own. She looked at the clocks on display, admiring them all, and noticed the little cuckoo clock. How could she miss it with the singing the cuckoo was making! Fearing the loss of another customer the Niece tried to explain. The clock had a defect but it was of sentimental value to her. She would make sure any clock she made for the Wise Woman would not behave in this way. The Wise Woman was intrigued and asked the story of the clock. She listened very carefully and then offered some advice.

"The cuckoo is afraid. He spent a long time in loneliness and darkness; he fears ending up back there. He cannot help but make sure that you are noticing him."

"But," said the Niece, "it is the endless singing that is making it so hard for me; I am noticing him, how could I not? But this is going to force me to remove the spring. What he fears will come true if he cannot reduce his singing."

"And isn't that sad?" said the Wise Woman. "You both want the same thing, but the cuckoo's fear is going to come between you and you will both be lost to each other. You cannot make him stop singing – no pleading, threats or anger from you will make that happen. All you can offer is your predictable presence. Over time he will come to believe in this and only then will the singing reduce."

The Niece thought hard and then smiled. She fetched some wood and carved on it a message to hang beside the cuckoo clock. The notice read:

> Please stop and admire this clock. It is the finest cuckoo clock you will ever see, made for me by my Uncle. It is also unique. The only cuckoo clock in the world that can sing every five minutes; there will never be another like it. This clock will

always be with me. I hope I can make for you a clock that you can equally hold dear, even though your clock will not chime so frequently.

People travelled far and wide to see the unique cuckoo clock. They placed orders for their own clocks and the Niece's own fame spread. The cuckoo could relax, sure now of the Niece's love for him; gradually the constant singing stopped. It became a conventional cuckoo clock. The Niece didn't need the notice any more, but her ordinary cuckoo clock would always be extraordinary to her.

Story 12

The Space Boy

Story type: Trauma, with elements of Life story and Therapeutic

Themes: Living with domestic violence; Impact of trauma; Hyperactivity to cope with fears

Age range: 7–12 years

Children who have been born into an atmosphere of fighting and domestic violence develop in a very different way from children who are born into calm and gentle homes. Their brains are biased to notice danger. This begins in the very earliest weeks. The parents, already in a state of stress and fear themselves, are not available to soothe and comfort their infant when she becomes aroused. In fact, the child's distress can trigger further fear within the parents, leading them into a defensive rather than an open and engaged state. They are not available to meet their child's needs. Instead of being an external regulator for the child facilitating the child's developing abilities for emotional regulation, these parents remain dysregulated themselves. In addition, their own focus on danger means that they cannot be mind-minded towards their child. They are poor at observing their child and making sense of her behaviours by understanding her internal emotional experience. The child experiences fear, worry and anxiety, but the parent cannot name, make sense of or help her with this. Instead of being soothed and settled, the child is wired for danger. The warning systems in her brain are on high alert so that as she grows she remains hypervigilant to any possible dangers, ready to go into a fight/flight reaction to even the most innocuous of cues.

The children experiencing such a lack of nurture early in life therefore develop with poor emotional regulation capacity. They cannot soothe these high alert states; neither are they able to relate to others so that other people can help them.

Difficulties with emotional regulation also interfere with the development of thinking, in particular the ability to perspective-take. Without this ability children are left with difficulties understanding their own or others' mental states – what they are thinking, feeling, believing and wishing for. Children are unable to make sense of their own internal experience because of this compromised ability to mentalize. They are left experiencing stress and fear, but unable to understand or soothe this.

The children are in a constant state of fear and tension. Their lack of interpersonal relatedness means that they are also left trying to manage this by themselves. They demonstrate poorly developed self-reliant behaviours alternating with attention-needing behaviours. In other words, the children are disorganized in their behaviours, both seeking and rejecting comfort, whilst their bodies remain continually ready for action. The children hide away their need for comfort and protection, their thirst to explore and learn in the world. Trusting no one, their expressed need is for control as they desperately try to draw upon their own resources to feel safe. These children cannot settle, focus or concentrate, especially as their stress increases. Even small increases in stress can lead to large reactions, and others are left 'walking on eggshells' as they anticipate the next outburst or meltdown.

This next story was written for a boy who had experienced a large amount of domestic violence before he was removed from his family into foster care and ultimately adopted. Whilst he has developed some security with his parents over time, he continues to struggle when away from them. This makes school a hugely stressful experience. In addition, his stress tolerance is very poor, so that even small increases in stress lead to major reactions. He finds it hard to tolerate his parents losing their attention on him, even for short periods. He struggles to share their attention with his siblings, to let his parents go out without him or even not knowing what they are doing whilst he is at school. Despite this constant need for their attention, he does not know how to let them help him to feel soothed or calmed. He remains emotionally disorganized, but in the absence of a feeling of emotional connection to his family, he is left trying to deal with this emotional experience by himself. His hypervigilance supported by a highly alert alarm system and quick movement into a state of fight or flight makes him a very challenging child to parent.

The Space Boy

This is a story about a boy. His name was Robert and long ago he lived on a distant planet. This was a sad time for Robert, for no one cared about him and all his family fought and squabbled amongst themselves. In fact, they were so busy fighting and squabbling that they quite forgot that they had a tiny boy in their family. When it all got too much for him, Robert would slip out of the door to a secret place he knew. He would lie on his back and look up into the sky. He would look at the stars and dream about being a space boy, flying from planet to planet.

Whilst he liked imagining being a space boy, this did not stop the fighting and squabbling at home. In fact, it just seemed to get worse. Robert did not care for this at all, so one day he set off all by himself to explore the world. He felt very brave as he strode off across the fields, but his bravery did not last for long. There were so many strange sounds around him, sounds of birds and the wind in the trees. Now you might think what is so scary about that, the birds and the wind won't hurt a little child, but Robert had grown up with sounds of fighting and squabbling, not with the sounds of the birds and the wind. He found himself missing the sounds he was so used to, even though they were scary as well. He thought about turning around and returning home, but the truth was he had wandered so far that he no longer knew if he could find his home again, and of course, no one was out looking for him as no one had noticed that he had gone.

At last, just as the sun was setting and a gloom was settling all around, Robert arrived at the edge of a deep and dark wood. He hesitated, not sure that he wanted to enter. He was feeling hungry and tired after his day of walking and was unsure what to do next. He sat down at the edge of the wood whilst he made up his mind. Well, strange as it was, and as scared as he was feeling, Robert was also very tired; before he knew it, he had fallen asleep, right there, on the soft grass between the fields and the woods, and who knew what would have become of him but for a strange turn of events. It so happened that this field was the perfect landing site for Mr and Mrs Frankum. They were explorers who, together with their son Tom, lived in a space ship and spent their time seeking their fortune in space. They flew from planet to planet, exploring the different worlds and trading with the many people they met.

Robert was awoken by the noise and disturbance of the spaceship landing. He could not believe his eyes as a door in the spaceship slowly slid open. Out stepped the three strangest creatures he had ever seen. At least they looked strange to Robert, as he had never seen people in space suits before. As they looked around, Robert made up his mind. He did the bravest thing a little boy could ever do – he decided to go up and say hello to the space family. Ordinarily this is not a very sensible thing to do. Children should rely on their parents to keep them safe, and approaching strangers can lead to all sorts of dangers. Robert, however, did not have parents to keep him safe. He had no way of knowing whether it was safe or not, but talking to these people felt safer than staying on his own. Well, luckily for Robert, the Frankum family were kind; they could not believe their eyes when they saw such a tiny little boy. They removed their space helmets and asked him who he was and why he was here in this field, all alone. Robert was struck dumb by surprise and relief. He had quite expected to be chased by them, but instead he found himself being taken aboard the space ship and being given food and drink. This he gratefully took, having had nothing all day. Then, whether from exhaustion or just the strangeness of the day, he fell fast asleep again.

And so began the adventures of Robert Frankum, because yes, Robert became part of their family. He grew in their hearts as he grew bigger and stronger. Robert was happy in this family, travelling from planet to planet. He saw many strange sights and got used to many strange sounds, but always there was a part of him that worried. He could never quite stop listening for the fighting and the squabbling to begin again, or worrying that one day he might have to leave this family too. This made him very fidgety. They would land on a planet and set off to explore, and Robert would look around at all the new things and would listen to all the sounds, but it was hard to focus on any of this. He would just settle to making a list of all the plants and trees he could see when he would be distracted by the houses and other buildings in the towns. Instead he would start to draw the buildings when he would notice the children playing nearby. He would join their play but never quite got used to the games as his attention would be distracted once again. Poor Robert, he just could not settle and relax. His mum and dad and even Tom would try to help him settle to one thing, but he would start fidgeting again. And always, always, he would listen for the fighting and squabbling to start again. Always he would wait to be told that he could not stay if he could not settle. This made Robert very anxious. He became very bossy as he tried to feel less worried. He had to have things just so; he didn't want to be here, he wanted to be there; he didn't want to sit down, he wanted to stand up; he didn't want to stand up, he wanted to sit down; and sometimes he just did not know what he wanted and then he shouted and screamed at Mum and Dad, and even at Tom.

Poor Robert and poor Mum and Dad; they could see that Robert was growing in their heart, but it was hard for him to feel safe and secure with them. It was hard for him to enjoy doing new things or going to new places, and always, they knew he was waiting for the fighting and squabbling to start again.

Mr and Mrs Frankum thought very hard about how to help Robert; he was their son now and they wanted him to be happy. They talked to some wise people who knew about children who had lived in families where there was fighting and squabbling. They remembered the tiny little boy who had been brave enough to walk away and brave enough to find them. They thought about how alone that little boy had been and realized that Robert did not know how he could let a mum and dad help him to feel safe. He wanted them to be his parents but he did not know how to be a son. He had had no one when he was tiny; he had never learned how to seek what he needed from parents. They made a plan. They decided that they would show Robert how he could be safe with them. They settled their space ship down on a planet where the people were kind and work was plentiful, and then they had lots of time to help Robert.

Kindly and gently, Mum and Dad showed Robert how to let them help him. When he became fidgety and could not stay in one place, they helped him to calm down. When he got cross and angry with them, they stayed with him. When he became anxious that the fighting and squabbling might start again, they let him know they understood he was scared. When Robert got bossy and demanding, they gently let him know that they were there and they could decide what was best for him.

Slowly, very slowly, Robert began to trust them. When he felt fidgety and unsettled he stayed close to Mum until he felt calmer. When he was cross and angry he let Mum hold him until he felt less cross, and when he was anxious that the fighting and squabbling might start again he learned to let Mum and Dad know so that they could reassure him. One day he was even able to tell them the scariest thing of all. He worried that he might have to leave them and be all on his own again. Then they held him and told him how sad they felt that he had such a big worry, how hard it was to fear that his family might not be forever and how sad that a little boy had left one family and now worried that he might lose this family too. No wonder he became anxious and cross when he had such a big worry.

And Robert found that his mum and dad, and Tom too, were always there. When he was fidgety, when he was bossy, when he was cross and angry, and when he didn't know what to do, he would look around and there they were, ready to help him. He learned to trust in their presence. He stopped listening for the fighting and squabbling to begin again, and do you know what? He even stopped worrying that one day he would have to leave this family. He had grown in their hearts and now he believed in his heart that they would always be there.

The Frankum family set off to explore space once more. They travelled from planet to planet in their space ship: Mum, Dad, Tom and Robert. The space boy had found his dream and he grew big and strong and as clever as any boy could be.

Notes about Part IV

Within Part III, attention was given to the children with an avoidant style of relating – self-reliance rather than connection, and independence rather than dependence, provides a measure of safety and security. The stories provided a way of opening the door on this emotional experience, facilitating emotional connection at a distance.

In this part, especially in the first two stories, the focus has been on children who present a different challenge to the parents trying to help them to feel safe and secure. These children will connect emotionally; they are able to be dependent, but do not want to explore independence. They are reactive to how they are feeling. They connect but don't want to let go – dependence overrides the desire for independence. They are driven by fears of not being good enough and of beliefs that they will be abandoned one day. Thus they cling to relationships through emotional displays, but leave little room for thought, either their own or of others. This makes it difficult to help these children find and notice the consistent or the predictable. Always reacting to emotional experience, the children fail to notice the responsive parenting that is available to them.

For these children the story can be a way of providing them with some thinking time. It can provide a structure and create some capacity for noticing the predictable and available caregiver who is trying to help them to feel safe. Connected through the act of storytelling, the child can relax and begin to find a point of trust that the caregiver does understand her, can accept her fears, doubts and worries, and will remain available to her.

Within the therapy room the containment provided by the routines of the session can be a starting point to help the child relax enough to notice the parents' availability. As the endless anxiety reduces a little, the child may be receptive to a story that voices her deepest fears and builds hope that consistent, predictable care can be available for her.

The third story in this part explores children who cannot find any security in either self-reliant or attention-needing styles of relating. Instead they develop a disorganized and controlling pattern of relating. They want but cannot seek the support of parents. These children have a reduced capacity for emotional regulation or for mentalization; they struggle to manage their emotional experience or to reflect upon this.

The story can provide a structure, rhythm and familiarity which can begin to soothe the over-aroused nervous system and allow the child some space for reflection, helped by the calm presence of their parent. In other words, storytelling can be an important tool for helping the child to learn to be with the parent. The child then becomes more open to co-regulation of her emotional state. Parent and child can then think together about the child's experience. The use of stories facilitates the development of increased capacity for regulation and for reflection.

Part V
LEARNING ABOUT RELATIONSHIPS

Story 13

Survival of the Fittest

Story type: Life story; Insight

Themes: Experience of neglect; Sibling relationships; Living with jealousy and fear; Needing to feel special

Age range: 9–16 years

Children learn about relationships from birth. The relationships that they are born into provide them with their earliest experience of relating with others. This learning will then stay with them as they grow and move out into the world. As they encounter new relationships, these early lessons guide their expectations and inform them about how to respond. The children remember the past, and this past guides their present and informs their future.

Sometimes the early relationships provide a good experience for the children and they grow up emotionally healthy and resilient. They go on to meet a range of people and develop relationships, some successful and others less so. The children navigate this varied experience successfully, their early experience staying with them and giving them the confidence to know that they are loveable, and of interest to others. If a current relationship appears to disconfirm this, they have the inner confidence to move on, to seek relationships that are better for them.

When the early relationships do not provide this secure start in life the children will have a much harder time. They will remain distrustful, seeking reassurance from others or trying to manage on their own. When they meet good, healthy relationships they remain anxious and uncertain, doubting the sincerity of the other, or waiting to be found lacking. In the process they lose what is being offered to them. The children might even try to provoke anger or frustration because this feels more in tune with how they experience themselves. When they meet poor relationships they feel that this is what they deserve, often staying with these relationships despite the pain they provide.

These children need unconditional love and support, to discover that they are loved in all their colours and moods. They anticipate conditional love. They try to be good in order to maintain this love. However, they are quick to despair when they find themselves getting something wrong or experiencing negative emotion. In response they behave in ways that appear highly troubled and are difficult to live with – deceit, stealing and hurting others all make it difficult for the parents to remain empathic, available and nurturing for the child. The child's worst fears appear confirmed as parents retreat from the hurt they experience in parenting this child. The child fearing the worst can become aggressive, wielding knives and hitting, punching and kicking. She might run away or turn her anger upon herself as she engages in self-harming behaviours, demonstrating to others how she feels about herself.

For these children periods of calm are interspersed with periods of highly troubled behaviours. The children believe their own history, confirmed by these current behaviours. They cannot believe in the love of their parents and they experience intense jealousy towards siblings who they fear have a larger portion of their parents' hearts.

This next story was written for a very bright, charming, delightful boy aged nine. Early experience with a highly punitive father and neglectful mother had led him to develop a propensity to hide his emotions, to appear happy and to try to take care of and please others. These fragile skills, however, were easily lost to him when his level of stress increased. He became convinced of his own sense of badness, certain that he would lose his adoptive family and convinced that they favoured his brother over him. He would become impulsive, acting without thinking. His fear increased when he found his parents treating him and his brother equally. This young boy had a deep belief that only one of them could be special within the family, and he quickly despaired if he thought that it was not him. This story was written as part of our exploration of his relationship with his brother, and as we gained an understanding of some of the more challenging behaviours that he could display.

Survival of the Fittest

This is a tale of long ago and far away. It is a story of brothers and the difficulties that can arise between them. Although it happened many years ago, I think it is a story that will resonate with brothers (and sisters) everywhere.

Deep in the freshwater swamps of East Africa lived Mr and Mrs Shoebill and their two young chicks, Jack and Joe. Jack was the eldest by a few hours. He was the bigger and stronger of the two chicks. Joe was small and weak at birth, and lack of care from his parents only made this fragility worse.

Mr and Mrs Shoebill were not the most attentive of parents. They would go hunting, leaving the chicks unguarded. Sometimes they remembered to bring back food, but often as not they forgot. The chicks would be left to fend for themselves. Jack, the stronger chick, would often pick on little Joe, pecking him violently and pushing him away from the nesting area. Their parents, noticing this show of strength, would then favour Jack. They provided him with food and water, letting Joe go without.

"You are strong Jack, you will survive. We will take care of you but not your brother," his parents would tell him.

Joe, seeing this, would sink further down into himself; he tried to shelter underneath his mother, but she would look at him with disdain. Instead of giving him shelter she would go to fetch water in her large bill to provide for her first-born. Similarly Mr Shoebill would fetch a large catfish, and after digesting it would regurgitate some for Jack but none was given to Joe. Although more attentive to him than Joe, Jack would also get the sharp end of Mr Shoebill's beak. He would be chided for not being strong enough, for not being clever enough, for needing to be taken care of. Desperate for favour, Jack would redouble his efforts to pick on Joe to prove his strength and worth to his neglectful parents.

And so things continued; somehow Joe clung to life, although he was weaker every day. He managed to get a little water from the vegetation around him and this sustained him – just. Then one fine morning, the chicks woke to find Mrs Shoebill gone and Mr Shoebill in a foul mood. He turned on Joe and shoved him out of the way; then turning to Jack, he berated him for not being big and strong enough. "It is your fault your mother has gone. She tells me I don't produce fine and strong chicks and she has gone to seek her fortune elsewhere. It is your fault; if you were bigger she would stay." At that he stalked off, leaving his young fledglings to fend for themselves. They did not know when he would return, but as like as not, he would be away for days. They were too young to be left so long; not yet able to get their own food they were weakening hour by hour. Joe especially would not survive another day.

And so things would have come to a sad ending if it were not for a stroke of luck. Although well hidden in the swamp there happened to pass close by Mr and Mrs Hamerkop.

Let me tell you about these noble birds. Whilst they had built many a nest each as fine and big as the last, and though they laid as many as seven eggs in a number of these nests, never had an egg hatched. It was so sad that this dedicated pair did not have a chick between them.

Mr and Mrs Hamerkop had just finished building their latest nest; this was a magnificent construction of 10,000 sticks carefully constructed in the fork of a tree. It was carefully positioned to hang over water and had been decorated with brightly coloured objects and plastic bottle tops, making it glint in the sun. Tired from their exertions and sad to see such a fine nest without the chance of a chick in it, they set out in search of food – a fish, shrimp or tasty frog to provide a little supper before they settled down to rest. They had strayed a little further than they had meant to, tempted by the freshwater swamp nearby, and that is how they came to notice Jack standing still and quiet close to some dense vegetation. He was so statue-like they may not have noticed him at all but for the quick, violent strike he made at the vegetation just as they were passing. It was futile; too young for catching fish, he came away empty-billed, but it was enough to attract the attention of Mr and Mrs Hamerkop.

"Why are you all alone there?" asked Mrs Hamerkop. "Surely you are too young to be feeding yourself?"

Jack explained that his father was away hunting and his mother had left them. Mrs Hamerkop looked at the bedraggled young bird and knew that he was not well cared for. She turned to her husband and pleaded with him.

"We have a nest standing empty; there is room enough for this young fellow, so let us take him home. We will help him to grow big and strong."

After just a little persuasion it was agreed and Jack was told to follow them back the way they had come. They were just leaving the edge of their nesting area when Mrs Hamerkop caught a glint of something at the edge of her vision. She slowed.

"Are there any more of you?" she asked young Jack. "Oh no," he said, "only me."

But there was something in the look he gave her that made Mrs Hamerkop pause. She looked more closely and of course saw a smaller and even more bedraggled chick, this one close to death. With a penetrating look at Jack, she gently picked him up in her dark, curved beak.

Jack protested, "I am the strong one. Joe is no use," but it was no good, they would not listen to him. With a heavy heart he followed the Hamerkops. Slower now, they continued with their journey, finally making it back to their nesting area. With some small effort both chicks were brought safely into the nest, and food and water supplied for them.

This was a time of great trial for Jack. He did not understand why the Hamerkops paid such close attention to Joe, giving him the tastiest morsels and making sure he had warmth and water. Jack was the strongest; why did they not give him such attention? True, he was given sufficient food, and even some flying lessons when Mr Hamerkop could spare the time, but always he noticed the greatest attention was given to Joe. Jack tried to show off his strength and prowess. As his flying got stronger he accompanied his new dad in search of food, but whatever he did, still the attention was given to Joe.

Jack remembered the words of his father; it was his fault his mother had left. Now maybe these new parents felt the same way. Maybe they saw malice in his soul, that he was a bad chick and one day they would send him away. It was just a matter of time. Sometimes his anger would flare as these fears grew inside of him. He would shout and huff, threatening them with his sharp straw-coloured bill. Then, afraid, he would take off, finding some swampy bit of marsh to stand in. Whilst he stood motionless he would remember that he had his chance to be special, to be the favoured one, that he had failed and now Joe had taken his place. At these times Mr Hamerkop would come and find him, gently guiding him back to the nest, finding the odd insect or sometimes a small rodent on the way. Jack would fly back into the nest and, finding a corner on the far side, would brood on his fate. Always eating away at him was the fear that, no longer special, he would one day have to leave and fend for himself.

All this time Joe was making slow progress, growing bigger and sturdier. He was not yet ready to fly but was thriving on the tender care and attention of his new and nurturing mother. Jack noticed Joe's plumage coming back, the feathers beginning to take on the blue-grey appearance of the adult Shoebill. Slowly but surely Jack's jealousy and fear grew. He tried to be a good son, to help where he could, to grow tall and strong, but always he would cast a look at Joe and fancy that he was getting bigger and stronger than him. Soon his fragile place in this family would be lost and Joe would grow up the pride of his adoptive parents.

Mr and Mrs Hamerkop did not understand what was eating at Jack; they did their best to care for both chicks, unaware that the attention they gave to Joe only made Jack feel more insecure. The Hamerkops were a species of bird that cared for all their young, helping them to grow to maturity. They were unaware that their close cousins were very different in their attitudes to parenthood. Shoebills invest in their strongest chick, leaving the younger to fail. They were unaware that Jack's insecurity was founded on an instinctive knowledge that only one chick could survive. Not understanding this they were not able to empathize with Jack's fears or to help him understand that two could be special in their family. Each of them had different needs – whilst Joe needed time, extra food and shelter, Jack was ready to test his wings, learn to fly and discover how to find food and water. Fairness for the Hamerkops was giving each son what he needed. They attended to their two adopted sons' varying needs, unaware that this very difference was eating away at Jack, leaving him aggressive and isolated.

This all came to a head one day when the two young fledglings were left alone whilst the parents went foraging. Joe was standing up tall and erect, testing his strength and spreading his wings. Jack saw the strength and beauty of his brother and the fear inside of him burst through. He flew at Joe, stabbing at him with his sharp beak. Joe did his best to dodge this ferocious attack. Who knows how this would have ended if it had not been for the chance that a neighbour was flying close by. Hearing signs of the struggle she came down and intervened in the attack. Jack, ashamed of what had occurred, and sure now that he was no longer welcome, flew away to the marsh. He found a hiding place where he could nurse his inner wounds, just as Joe was having his own external, but fortunately superficial, wounds attended to.

When Mr and Mrs Hamerkop returned, they were distressed to find out what had occurred in their absence. They despaired for their eldest son, and worried what the impact would be on the younger of the two. They thanked their neighbour profusely for helping out and wondered with her what they should do. Now this neighbour was wise in the way of birds. She understood the different nesting habits of the two species and had some inkling about what was troubling Jack. She shared her thoughts with the two distraught parents, wondering if Jack maybe needed his parents to understand his darkest fears. She offered to stay with Joe whilst the two of them went off to find their errant son.

It took them some time to find Jack. They checked out his favourite spots but could see no sign of him. Mrs Hamerkop feared the coming of night and what would happen if they did not find him in time. Further and further they hunted until at last, just as they were beginning to despair, they spotted him. Alone he stood, the picture of abject misery. Quietly they approached and gently tended to him. They brought him food and water and sheltered him as if he was a new-born chick. They stayed with him as the sun set and the air chilled. They spoke soft words, of their love for him, their need for his strength and courage and their understanding of his fear. They had not understood how much he feared losing his special status, but now they did. Both chicks were special to them, that is how it was in this family, but they understood now how scary this was for Jack. He had so little care from the birds that hatched him, how could he know that there was enough for both of them now? Jack was amazed; he was being welcomed back to the nest despite what he had done. His fears made sense; his need to be special was understood. Maybe, just maybe, he could stay and share this family with his brother.

And so Jack returned with his understanding parents. He continued to grow strong and handsome. It was not plain flying though; some days the old worries and anger would re-emerge, but always his parents would be there, helping him through these darker times.

They became a fine pair, the Shoebill brothers who both survived, and they went on to raise families of their own. For generations after, the descendants of Jack and Joe would raise both their chicks even though the practice amongst the rest of the Shoebills remained to nurture only one. A special affinity developed between the Shoebills and the Hamerkops despite their differences, and they continue to look out for each other, even to this day. Survival of the fittest may work in the harsh terrain of East Africa, but sometimes recognizing the specialness within the differences can produce a strength all of its own.

Story 14

A Mummy Finds Out How to Look After Her Baby

Story type: Insight; Solution

Themes: Experience of neglect; Mummies and babies; The comfort of nurture; Learning about relationships

Age range: 5–12 years

Children who have experienced neglect or abuse can struggle to make sense of this. Whilst living within their birth families this is just the norm, the way things are. The children may not question it or expect anything to be different. Removing children from these family environments is the most drastic intervention that the state can make. Children are provided with a new family or, in many cases, a series of new families. This might be in foster care, adoptive families or with members of the extended birth family. Some children may move to residential care when they are older. All of these environments offer different ways of being part of a family. Children have to adjust to different family and cultural practices, they have to understand different sets of family rules and they have to learn to love and feel secure with alternative parents. These changes and differences can present considerable challenges to the children, and not least of these challenges is making sense of their past and current experience.

Life story work is one way that social workers, parents and others try to help the children gain this understanding and resolve any confusion they have about what has happened and is happening to them. Whilst this practice varies, there is now a greater understanding about the work that is needed, work that starts rather than ends with the familiar 'life story book'. This book provides the children with a story of their life experience. Photographs and facts are collected and presented to the children matched to their current developmental age.

Some creative people go beyond a simple book – memory boxes and other creative ways of preserving the children's histories can provide a very tangible connection to the past. The exploration of life story must not end with these materials, however. They are static, fixed in a point of time tailored to the child's level of understanding. For all of us the exploration of life story is something that occurs throughout life, perhaps triggered by life events or increased maturity. Children and adults are constantly revisiting their past and developing a fresh understanding of this. The children need information and help to make sense of this information.

This is an ongoing process; children need support as they express curiosity or even distress about their past life. The children can have very concrete beliefs about what has happened to them, supported by varying levels of explicit memory about their earlier experiences. Alongside the memories they can bring to mind the children also have implicit memories; these are memories of early experience that are out of consciousness. The children remember without knowing that they remember. These unconscious memories can be a powerful driver of behaviour. For example, imagine a simple event such as someone raising their hand to wave. This could trigger an implicit memory of being hit by an adult. Without understanding why, the child experiences a surge of anxiety and moves into a state of readiness, either attacking or running from the perplexed hand waver. Understanding something of their early experience can help children to be more flexible in their responses. With increased ability to reflect, and understand, unconscious triggers can be understood and actions overridden.

Stories can be a helpful way of helping children to understand their own early experiences, and to make sense of and resolve some of the confusions that they hold. Examples of such stories can be found in the first part of this book. The next story demonstrates another use of story, not only to convey facts about life experience and to support transition and permanence, but also to aid understanding about why things happened as they did. This story was written for a young girl living in foster care. She was eight years old when this was written, although a degree of learning difficulty and emotional immaturity meant that, developmentally, she was younger. This young girl was struggling to understand the difference between her two mummies. She often confused them in her mind, so that her foster mummy and her birth mummy merged. She had a sense of vulnerability about her birth mummy, wanting to go 'home' and take care of her, but also confusion about why her birth mummy had behaved towards her in such a neglectful way. She worried that she was naughty, and that was why her birth mummy had stopped taking care of her. Of course this worry made her feel highly insecure with her foster mummy – perhaps this mummy would find her to be too naughty as well. This story was written to help this girl make some sense about why her mummy had not taken care of her very well, and also to provide a sense of hope that things could be different in her now permanent foster home. I wanted the story to convey a sense of being able to trust in warm, nurturing care. This would allow the child to feel more secure with her foster mummy, but also symbolically to give her a sense of the neglected baby still within her being taken care of.

A Mummy Finds Out How to Look After Her Baby

(This story first appeared in K.S. Golding and D.A. Hughes (2012) *Creating Loving Attachments: Parenting with PACE to Nurture Confidence and Security in the Troubled Child*. London: Jessica Kingsley Publishers.)

Once upon a time there was a mummy. She was a new mummy. She had never had a baby before. She wanted to look after her new baby really, really well, but she had a problem. She was not sure how to look after her new baby. When the baby cried she was not sure what he needed. When he was content, she was not sure how to play with him.

The mummy was very worried about this. She tried to think back to when she was little. It was hard to remember when she was very small, but she knew her mummy had not looked after her very well.

The mummy decided she needed help. If she was going to be a good mummy she needed someone to teach her. Very carefully she wrapped her baby in a blanket and put him in his pram. She collected a few things she needed and set off to look for help.

The first person she met was another mummy. Surely another mummy would be able to help her? She showed the other mummy her baby and asked her: "How can I be a good mummy?" This mummy taught her what babies need – how to feed them, change them and play with them. She gave the mummy some nappies so that she could keep her baby clean and dry.

The mummy carried on her journey, thinking about what she had been told. Her baby woke up and cried. Carefully she changed the baby's nappy. Still the baby cried. She tried to feed the baby but he didn't want the milk. She tried to play with the baby, but he still cried. The mummy felt like crying too. She still couldn't be a good mummy.

Next the mummy met a nurse. She told the nurse about her baby and how he would not stop crying although she had done everything she had been told. The nurse picked the baby up and cuddled him. The baby stopped crying. The nurse showed the mummy how to rock the baby and pat him on the back to help him feel more comfortable. Then she helped the mummy feed her baby. Finally the baby fell asleep. The mummy thanked the nurse and carried on with her journey.

When the baby next woke the mummy carefully changed his nappy and fed him. She rocked him and patted him on the back. Then she laid him in his pram, but he didn't go to sleep. He started to fret. The mummy didn't know what to do.

The mummy met a woodcarver. This man was a grandfather. He told the mummy that when his grandchildren came to stay they liked to play with rattles that he had carved out of wood. He gave the mummy a rattle he had made. The mummy showed the rattle to the baby and he smiled.

The mummy walked on. She thought about all the things she had learned about looking after babies – how to feed them and change them, how to pat them on the back so they felt more comfortable and how to play with them. Still she was worried. How would she know what her baby needed? When should she feed him or change him? When did he need rocking and when did he need playing with? The mummy had learned how to look after her baby; she understood this in her head; but deep in her heart, though, this mummy still struggled. The head learns by being taught; the heart learns by being loved. The mummy needed head and heart. She needed to be taught and to be loved.

The mummy felt tired and cold. She had walked a long way from home and felt too weary for the journey back. She did not know it but she had walked so far that she was near to the home of her fairy godmother, and her fairy godmother found her. She didn't say a word, just took her in her arms and cuddled her. She took her inside her house and sat her by the warm fire. Whilst the mummy was resting and getting warm again, the fairy godmother took care of the baby. She then made the mummy some warm buttered toast.

As the mummy ate the toast she felt better. She started to ask her fairy godmother how to look after babies. The fairy godmother put her finger to her lips. "No more questions," she said. "Let me take care of you and you will be able to look after your baby."

Over the next few weeks the mummy stayed with her fairy godmother. She enjoyed being taken care of. Her fairy godmother ran her baths, and made her meals. Sometimes they played games. When she felt sad or worried her fairy godmother gave her a cuddle and helped her to feel better. Gradually the mummy began feeling more confident about taking care of her baby. She found that she knew when her baby needed feeding, changing, rocking or playing with. The mummy was puzzled. Her fairy godmother had not taught her about looking after her baby but she found she could do it. "How do I know what to do?" she asked. The fairy godmother told her: "Your head knew what to do, but you also need your heart to look after your baby. The answers in your heart have helped you to use the answers in your head." The mummy looked puzzled. "But how has my heart learned?" she asked. The fairy godmother laughed. "No more questions," she said. "Remember, just let me take care of you, and you will be able to look after your baby."

Story 15

Sally Sunshine and the Big Bag of Worries

Story type: Therapeutic

Themes: Experience of lots of worries; Managing fears; Developing self-reliance

Age range: 5–12 years

'A problem shared is a problem halved', or so the well-known saying goes. For children who find it difficult to trust others, this is not a motto that they can believe in. They have many worries, difficult beliefs and expectations that they carry around with them. They lock these worries away, afraid that if they let others know, they will be revealing something bad or defective about themselves. If this happens, they will be abandoned all over again. Of course the weight of the worries double when they are left untended. The children try to ignore the worries, but their behaviour betrays them. When a child can't communicate in words, the communication is made unconsciously through angry, rejecting or in other ways challenging behaviour. This very behaviour becomes another burden as the belief that they are bad is further confirmed for the child.

Therapy is often seen as an answer to help the child who appears emotionally distressed and who is not experiencing the security in the family that was hoped for. This, however, presents a further challenge to the child. A kind, sympathetic therapist can trigger a further range of worries. The child fears trusting the therapist just as she feared trusting the parent – revealing herself in all her worries presents a vulnerability that she was trying to hide. Whilst we understand the power of relationships to heal, the child fears these relationships, believing that they too will hurt, punish and reject. Therapy is resisted and the therapeutic process is avoided.

The children need help but this will take time. No quick fixes —
therapist and parent need to work together and with the children,
building engagement and safety. This can lead the children gently into
relationships within which they can dare to be vulnerable. Only then
will the resistance fade away so that the children are able to use the
relationships to make sense of their struggles, and to share their worries.

I owe my thanks for the next story to Virginia Ironside for her
inspiring story, *The Huge Bag of Worries* (Ironside 1996). I could not
improve on this image and therefore borrowed it for a story written for
a young girl who found it very difficult to share her worries with me.

Sally Sunshine and the Big Bag of Worries

Once upon a time there was a young girl. She was ten years old and
she was called Sally Sunshine. When she was happy she was just
like her name, full of sunshine. She was kind and helpful and full
of fun.

But Sally had lots of worries and then a cloud would come out
and block the sun. Sally would get grumpy and cross.

It was very hard to help Sally with her worries because she kept
them in a bag that she carried around with her. You could not see the
bag, but it was there. The bigger the worries, the heavier the bag;
the heavier the bag, the more cross and grumpy Sally got.

Sally lived with foster parents. Her foster mum and dad tried to
help her with her worries, but it was difficult because they were deep
inside the bag. Sometimes they guessed what the worries might be.

They guessed that she was finding her work hard at school, and
they tried to help her with it.

They guessed that she was feeling cross with her brother, and
they tried to help her feel better.

They guessed that she was missing her friend who had moved a
long way away, and they tried to comfort her.

They guessed that she was missing her mummy, and they would
tell her when the next contact would be.

Now all this helped a little bit, but the bag of worries was still
very heavy and Sally still got cross and grumpy.

Sally had a friend, Karen, who would visit and try to help her with her worries. Karen was called a therapist. She wanted Sally to open the bag and take out the worries and talk about them. This really frightened Sally because there were some big worries in there that she did not want to talk about. She felt very cross with Karen when she wanted to get these worries out. This gave her another worry. She worried that Karen might not want to come and see her again because she was cross. This worry went in the bag as well, and the bag got heavier.

One day the bag of worries was really heavy, and Sally was feeling very cross and grumpy. A big cloud was covering the sunshine. Sally got cross with her foster mummy. Sally got cross with her brother. She even got cross with the family dog. Sally stomped up to her bedroom. She sat on the bed, the big bag of worries beside her. Sally did not know what to do. She wanted the sunshine to come back, but the bag was so heavy.

Now this day was a magical day. Magical days don't happen very often, but when they do, wonderful things can happen. Sally had a doll, Joanne, who was very special. She had always been with Sally. On this very magical day Joanne was able to talk. What a surprise Sally had when Joanne spoke to her! She told Sally that she shared her worries with Joanne.

THEY WERE HER WORRIES TOO.

Suddenly the bag felt just a little bit lighter. Joanne asked Sally to be really brave, and look at the worries with her. Sally wasn't sure, but she took a deep breath and together they got the worries out one by one.

First they took out the worry about not being able to do schoolwork. Sally felt bad when she found reading hard. Joanne sympathized; it was horrible to think that you weren't good at something. It was scary, too, because you worry that you might never find it easy. Joanne squeezed Sally's hand and told her that it was hard learning to do things. She reminded her that she had lots of help with this at school and she was getting better and better at it.

Next they took out the worry about getting cross with her brother. Joanne laughed at this one. "Your brother can be very annoying; all sisters get cross with their brothers sometimes."

They took out the worry about missing her friend who had moved away. Joanne felt sad when she thought about this one. "Yes, it is sad when friends go away, but we can feel sad together and maybe that will help."

Now they came to the worry about missing Sally's mummy. This was a hard one to think about. Joanne cried when she thought about it. "We both miss your mummy," she said. "It is hard when a little girl can't live with her mummy. It is hard when your mummy doesn't know how to look after her little girl. It is confusing when the little girl grows up and doesn't need so much looking after, but she still can't live with her mummy."

Joanne thought hard and said: "You know what, even big girls need looking after sometimes, and I still don't think your mummy knows how to do this. I am so pleased that you have another mummy who knows all about looking after little girls and all about looking after big girls. She can keep us both safe."

Sally felt a bit better, but there were still some worries in the bag and the next one was even harder. She didn't know if she wanted to get this one out. Joanne said: "It's a magical day today, and I can talk to you. We have a chance to talk about this together, and remember, IT IS MY WORRY TOO!"

Sally took a deep breath and reached in to the bag. She pulled out the worry and said: "I worry that my mummy is on her own and now I am big I should be looking after her."

"Yes," said Sally, "that is a big worry, isn't it? We like being taken care of here in this family. It feels nice being with a mummy and daddy who can keep us safe, but that does mean Mummy is on her own, with no children to take care of her. It's a big worry thinking about Mummy on her own."

Joanne looked at Sally and whispered: "Do you really think Mummy might want you to take care of her? Maybe she is pleased that you are being taken good care of here. Maybe she likes being with her cats. She knows how to look after the cats. She can do a good job looking after them."

Sally looked thoughtful. Maybe Mummy was pleased that she was being taken good care of, and they did see each other when it was contact time.

Joanne hugged Sally tight. "We have looked at so many worries. You are being so brave, but there is one worry left and it is the biggest of all."

Sally took a big gulp. Yes, she did not want to talk about this one.

Joanne looked at her and said: "Remember, IT IS MY WORRY TOO!"

Joanne reached into the bag and brought out the worry. "We worry," she said, "that when all these worries make us cross and grumpy it means we are bad. Maybe we are so bad that no one will want to look after us."

Sally could feel herself getting cross and grumpy; she wanted to shout at Joanne to go away. This was too scary to think about. Joanne held her hand tight and said: "You are being so brave. This is a very big worry isn't it? I can share it with you. IT IS MY WORRY TOO. How hard it is to worry about getting cross and grumpy. We try so hard but still it happens, and then we worry that maybe people won't like us any more. They may not understand that it is an accident, that we don't mean to be so cross, but we are worried about school and friends and Mummy; with all these worries, it is so hard not to be cross and grumpy. But you know what – our foster mummy and daddy are still looking after us, even though we are sometimes cross and grumpy with them. They don't think we are bad. We get cross and grumpy with Karen and she told us that she didn't mind. She still comes to see us. She doesn't stop liking us."

Sally thought hard about this. She still wasn't sure, but she was wondering about it.

Joanne told her that the worries weren't all going to go away at once, but to remember that she would always be there to share them. "I won't always be able to talk to you, but you will always know that you can share these worries because THEY ARE MY WORRIES TOO."

Sally Sunshine picked up the bag of worries. It felt a lot lighter now. A cloud had lifted and she could feel sunshine coming back into the room. The bag would get heavy again, but Joanne would always be there to share the worries with her. She could also share the worries with her foster mum and dad, and with Karen. Maybe one day she would be brave enough to share the really big worries with them as well.

"Yes," said Joanne, "and when you get the worries out and share them, the bag will feel lighter and you won't feel so cross and grumpy. Sally Sunshine, you will be just like your name, full of sunshine."

Notes about Part V

The stories in this part provide three different examples about how stories can be used to help children understand and manage relationships, whether this is with parents, siblings or therapists. Learning to relate to family, and to adults offering help and support, provides an important foundation for managing the complex world of friendships and peer relationships.

When children are struggling with peer relationships, getting into conflictual relationships, becoming socially isolated or moving quickly from potential friend to friend, they can be helped to develop more pro-social abilities. This might be through social skills groups, circle time in school or programmes such as anger management. For children with a secure foundation within their family these interventions can be helpful. These interventions can fail, however, when the children have not yet learned to trust and depend upon the close adults in their lives.

Thus the child who is rivalrous with his sibling, fearing that he will be favoured, is likely to also find it difficult to develop friendships without similar fears that his friend might be better than him in some way. He may be very prone to feeling hurt or rejected by even the normal and ordinary conflicts of friendship. Instead of being able to resolve these, he may engage in some sort of revenge on these friends, thus damaging potential friendships further.

These children are at an additional disadvantage when they find it hard to trust the adults in their lives to support them with these childhood struggles. Struggling to believe in a foster mother when you can't understand why your birth mother did not look after you properly can lead to difficulties in letting parents or indeed therapists support you with the emotional difficulties being experienced. As explored earlier in this book, these children can end up trying to go it alone, struggling to manage an increasingly complex world without the foundation of security and support to draw upon.

It is therefore important in supporting children with attachment difficulties to help them make sense of these struggles, to provide them with some insight about why relationship problems in the present can relate to relationship experience from earlier in their lives. This can then form a platform to help children to start to believe in their worthiness and to seek support when they need it.

The stories in this part were all used as part of this process. The story provided the children with an opportunity to reflect on their experience and thus to develop increased insight about why relationships are difficult as well as providing the possibility that it does not always need to be that way.

I have used such stories in various ways – reading them to children in therapeutic sessions, posting them to the child following sessions, or providing the story as part of a conclusion to my work with them. This latter is a way of summarizing what we have discovered in our journey together. In this way the stories become part of a bigger process within which the children are enabled to explore their experience in a variety of ways.

Part VI
STORIES FOR PARENTS

Story 16

A Daughter's Tale

Story type: Insight; Life story

Themes: Experience of life story; Fears of abandonment; Poor frustration tolerance

Age range: School-age children and their parents

The stories in this part have been written explicitly for parents. Storytelling is part of being human. There is no time in our history when humans have not told stories to each other. Stories can inform, entertain and elucidate. They are engaging, non-threatening and form an important part of the relationships we create with each other. Parenting advice can often sound critical, or invalidating of the parents' experience. Lectures, however sensitively given, can leave the parent with a sense of not being good enough or a feeling that they should have been doing a better job. Stories feel much more collaborative, a way of conveying understanding of the experience of the parent, and providing some ideas of different ways of helping the child that the parent might try, without implying that this is what they 'should' be doing.

This next story was written for a mother and her nine-year-old daughter. I wrote this in rhyme because the young girl had previously shown a delight in rhyming stories. I wanted to give some voice to her experience, as I understood it, and provide her with an opportunity of sharing this with her mother. Together, mother and daughter could more deeply understand the child's experience.

A Daughter's Tale

(This story first appeared in K.S. Golding (2014) *Nurturing Attachments Training Resource: Running Parenting Groups for Adoptive Parents and Foster or Kinship Carers*. London: Jessica Kingsley Publishers.)

Here is a tale of a girl, brave and true,

To look at her she's just like you,

But life has been hard and sometimes sad,

Read on and I'll tell you the good and the bad.

She was born to a mummy in a hard place,

Young, poor and worries that were hard to face,

She tried to cope but without even a home,

A baby was too much to care for alone.

This mummy was brave and knew it wouldn't do,

So she promised I'll find another family for you,

A mummy and daddy who have more than I,

The baby looked back and just asked: "Why?"

With tears in her eyes she tried to explain,

You deserve a life without such pain,

I cannot give you all that you need,

I must say goodbye, it has been agreed.

With help of others, a mum and dad were found,

A brother too, who wanted a sister around,

Be happy, birth mum said to her daughter,

Forgetting life is not only smooth water.

Now this story is happy and sad in part,

The girl grew strong and stout of heart,

Happy times there were, but sad times too,
Because life is a mixture that we all have to do.

The happy times were easy and full of fun,
She was loved and loved back, they lived in the sun,
But sad times were harder, the sun in the shade,
And memories of first mummy did not fade.

A question kept growing big in her mind,
I know this mum is strong, loving and kind,
But when it is difficult, and smiles are few,
I fear you are telling me I am too much for you?

A secret kept growing deep in her heart,
Maybe she could live with her family in part,
When Mummy was mean and life seemed unfair,
Her first mummy perhaps still could be there?

But there's a flaw in the plan, however clever,
Because all children need one family forever,
Whether happy or sad, and when times are tough
A family who stick with you when life is rough.

So Mummy understand, this girl's doing her best,
She smiles and she laughs, but needs a rest,
She needs to be sad, and to be angry too,
She needs to share fears of being too much for you.

If you can stay strong and hold her tight,
And keep her safe when she needs to fight,
This young girl will have a family to treasure,
And will know in her heart that this family's forever.

Story 17

William and Edward

Story type: Insight, with elements of Solution

Themes: Fears of rejection; Sibling relationships; Using PACE; Power of empathy

Age range: Adults

The next two stories were written explicitly for parents to help them have experience of parenting with a PACE attitude. PACE describes Playful parenting, with Acceptance of the child's inner world, Curiosity about the meaning underlying the behaviour and Empathy for the child's emotional state. This parenting attitude was suggested by Dan Hughes to help parents maintain emotional connection with their children (see Hughes 2009; see also Golding and Hughes 2012). Healthy emotional development relies on the experience of a parent who is attuned to the emotional experience of the child. Parents use their mentalizing skills, their ability to be mind-minded, to understand what a child is experiencing in the moment. They can then use this understanding to help the child with this emotional experience. The child gets an experience of being understood and loved unconditionally. Whatever he does or feels, the parents will still be there to take care of him. This is the basis of nurture and, combined with appropriate structure and boundaries matched to the developmental needs of the child, helps a child to feel safe and secure.

Adopting an attitude of PACE and maintaining this even in the most challenging of circumstances is not easy. Whilst playful parenting can be easy when the child and parent are enjoying their relationship, maintaining a playful stance at appropriate times, even when life is stressful, can be more challenging. In addition, the parent needs to understand and accept the child's inner world without trying to change or reinterpret this world for the child. This is how the child feels; it is neither right nor wrong, it just is. Such acceptance relies on curiosity about the meaning underlying the behaviour that the child is displaying. Whilst challenging behaviour must be contained and managed, only with acceptance and curiosity will parents be able to also maintain their empathy for the child's emotional state.

PACE is helpful for all children, but becomes more important when parenting children who are insecure. Secure children feel emotionally connected to their parents, and grow up knowing and believing in this connection. They know that they are loved unconditionally and that their parents are interested in their experience of the world. This security means that they can take structure, supervision and discipline in their stride. They may push against the boundaries and protest at the restrictions placed upon them, but in their heart they know that they are being loved and cared for. When parents use discipline and boundaries, the 'correction' part of parenting, the children already feel connected. Secure children will modify their behaviour in line with the consequences provided by their parents without doubting the parents' love and security.

Insecure children do not have this inner belief that they will be loved no matter what. They anticipate that love is conditional. Therefore they can mess up. They fear that one day the parent will abandon them as others have abandoned them in the past. They learn to behave in controlling, coercive and self-reliant ways as a way of protecting themselves from these fears. Thus their safety and security comes from their behaviours rather than from their connection with their parents. This is a fragile security that leads to increased disconnection from their parents. Short-term security is gained at the cost of long-term connection. To truly give the children a sense of long-term security the children need to be helped to believe in and enjoy emotional connection with their parents. PACE in parenting helps parents to provide this experience for the child.

This is not an easy approach to parenting. The children will resist emotional connection and will be distressed by boundaries and discipline. Connection and correction can both trigger fear in the insecure children. Whilst the children need PACE, they will also fight against it. This can leave the parent feeling rejected, helpless and with a sense of failure. Maintaining PACE until the child feels safe enough to trust in it can be a very long-term process. Parents need and deserve sensitive support to help them to stay with this process.

The following story was written as part of providing this support to parents caring for children with difficulties in attachment, children who fear connection with parents. The story appears in a group work programme for parents as a way of helping them to reflect on and understand PACE (see Golding 2014). It has a particular focus on the role of empathy within PACE, and how empathy comes out of curiosity and acceptance.

William and Edward

(This story first appeared in K.S. Golding (2014) *Nurturing Attachments Training Resource: Running Parenting Groups for Adoptive Parents and Foster or Kinship Carers.* London: Jessica Kingsley Publishers.)

Mandy and John have adopted ten-year-old Edward and his younger brother, William. Both boys spent their early years living with an emotionally absent mum, who was subject to domestic violence and was largely neglectful of the boys' needs. Their father was a bully who could be physically abusive to the boys as well as his partner. He was a strong disciplinarian with a sadistic edge to the punishments he gave out. He would be marginally easier on Edward than William, a 'favouritism' that Edward struggles to lose in his adoptive family. The boys were removed into care when they were four and three respectively. They lived in a foster placement for nine months before moving to live with Mandy and John.

It is a wet, miserable Sunday in November. The day had been fractious, with the boys being confined indoors because of the weather. Mandy breathes a sigh of relief as both boys have bathed and are in their pyjamas, ready for bed. She checks her watch; John should be back from checking on his elderly mother at any moment. She looks forward to the glass of wine they have promised themselves once both boys are settled. She sends Edward and William up to clean their teeth whilst she is preparing a parcel to send for her niece's birthday. She has just reached for the scissors to cut the tape when she hears a fight breaking out upstairs. With a groan she runs out into the hall just in time to witness Edward pushing William downstairs. She is powerless to help as she sees William bouncing from top to bottom.

"Edward!" she shouts angrily as she rushes to check on William.

Edward glares at her defiantly and then rushes downstairs past her and towards the front door. She notices him bend to pick up the scissors that she had dropped in her haste. Quickly she moves to block him from leaving the house. Edward kicks her deftly in the shin and, brandishing the scissors, lunges at her. Mandy moves out of the way and before she can do anything he is out of the house and away.

Mandy, feeling powerless to help Edward, goes to attend to her younger son. She texts John, asking him to hurry home. William is sitting up, conscious, but clearly in pain. She bends down to him and gently asks where it hurts. She is pretty sure his arm is broken. She helps him to his feet as John comes through the door. After a quick catch-up they agree that John will take William to the accident and emergency department of the nearby hospital whilst she goes out to look for Edward.

Mandy puts on her coat and picks up a torch and Edward's coat. She thinks through all the places he might have run to. She doesn't think he will have gone across the field in the dark, so instead she walks down the road towards the play park on the corner. As she approaches she shines her torch over the equipment, but her heart sinks when she can't see him anywhere. She stands still, thinking about where else he might be. A movement catches her eye in a nearby tree. Looking up she sees Edward perched precariously on one of the lower branches.

Moving across to the tree Mandy shouts up: "Come on Edward, we have to get you down."

Edward sees her and quickly climbs even higher. She sees his eyes reflected in the torchlight, wild with terror. She notices the glint of scissors still in his hand. Mandy stands stock still, the stillness belying the racing of her mind as she tries to think what to do.

Mandy can still see Edward in the tree, small and wild with panic. He appears to be oblivious to the rain soaking him to the skin, or to the shivering that is controlling his whole body. His eyes on his mother, he looks poised to move at any moment. Mandy thinks hard, but she is unsure what to do. Her shin throbs from the earlier kick, and in her mind's eye she can still see William bouncing down the stairs. She can feel the anger rising inside her, but knows that this will not help the situation.

Taking a deep breath, she calls quietly up to Edward, "It's okay Edward, I am here to help you. I'm not going to hurt you. I am going to wait until you are not feeling so scared and then I'll help you down from the tree."

The minutes seem like hours as Mandy waits without moving. She fears any movement on her part will panic Edward further. She watches him crouched in a higher branch; she doesn't know how much his shivering is from the cold or from the panic she sees reflected in his eyes. She knows he is not able to think in this state, but will react instinctively. She fears what he might do in his terror. She is still aware of the anger inside her. Why does he always spoil things, and why always his brother? William follows Edward everywhere, doting on him, but all he gets in return is this aggression.

Mandy thinks back to the boys who arrived on her doorstep five years ago: William, quiet and pale, and Edward, always ready for a fight, trying to appear tough and uncaring. She has experienced some breakthroughs with him over the years as he has allowed a more vulnerable needy side to show. He is starting to let her take care of him. Right now it feels like this progress was just a false hope. She looks up and watches him poised for action. This is how it has always been for Edward, waiting for the next beating, the next disappointment. In some ways he is so brave to keep on fighting;

uncomfortable as he is he will not give in. Even after five years he expects the worst. Mandy reflects on this. What is the worst that Edward keeps waiting for? Inside herself she knows the answer, although this knowledge is touched with her own sense of failure, and despair that she cannot reach this boy.

Edward still expects to be hurt. He knows in the core of his being that he is a bad child. His father had shown him this every day of his young life. His mother, in her inability to care for him, had reinforced this developing sense of self. Edward expects not to be loved; worse, he expects not to stay. He is waiting for them to give up on him.

Mandy slowly moves a little closer. She wonders how much time has passed. Quietly she speaks to Edward, her voice gentle and caring. She tells him it is okay, she will help him. This has been a difficult day but they will get through it. William is okay, Edward will be okay.

Edward glares down at her: "Go away, I hate you. You're a f****** bitch!"

Mandy steels herself to ignore this tirade; if she rises to it, all will be lost. "You are so angry right now. You hate us all. It feels like none of us are here for you, doesn't it? So cross and so scared. I am not going anywhere. We will get through this together."

Did she imagine it or has Edward relaxed slightly? She takes another step closer and repeats herself. She continues quietly reassuring him that they will get through this together. Yes, he definitely looks a little calmer. Quietly she calls up, "Drop the scissors Edward, let's get them out of the way."

With relief she sees him open his hand and the scissors clatter to the ground. Quietly and slowly she reaches down, picks them up and puts them in her pocket. She looks up again.

Edward is looking down at her. "I didn't mean to hurt him."

"I know, you were cross with him. It's okay, we can sort this."

"He had the toothpaste, I needed it."

Mandy groans inwardly; such a small thing but so big for Edward – small things telling him over and over again "you're not good enough." Having to be first, having to be special, or what?

"It is so scary for you, thinking we don't love you enough, that we don't want you. I am here. I will help you."

"Will I have to go? Now I have hurt William, am I leaving?"

"No, Edward. We are a family. We will get through this together. I am here. It will be all right."

"I'm cold!"

"Come on, let's get you out of the tree. I think it's another bath for you. We need to warm you up."

Edward stares down at his mother, uncertainty still in his eyes. Cautiously he moves, turning around on the branch and reaching with his foot for the branch beneath. Mandy holds her breath as she waits for him to get a little lower, waiting until she can reach up and help him.

"Move your foot to the left there, that will hold your weight."

Edward moves down another branch, almost within reach. Mandy guides him down one more branch and then she can reach him. Gently she holds him to her as he sobs quietly. "Come on, it's over now. Let's get home."

"Is he all right, William? Have I hurt him?" Mandy can see the fear and the sorrow in Edward's eyes.

She smiles and gently tells him: "He is okay. I think his arm may be broken. I have a feeling you are going to be carrying his bag for him for quite a while!" Edward smiles too. "I can help him. Until it's better I can do things for him! I am sorry, Mum."

"I know you are, Edward, I know."

Later she will weep, allowing herself to absorb the tension of this evening, and to feel some of the despair and failure that this little boy provokes in her, the fear that maybe they won't get through to him. For now it is enough that he is safe. Holding him to her, they walk back towards the house.

Story 18
Longing and Belonging

Story type: Insight, with elements of Solution

Themes: Exploring life story; Feelings of longing; Fear of rejection; Finding acceptance

Age range: Adults

I have worked with many parents, adopters, foster parents, kinship parents and residential parents who have embraced the idea of PACE and incorporate this into their parenting of children. I have witnessed their struggles to maintain this attitude in the face of the exceptional challenges that the children present to them. To stay believing in the importance of connecting with the child when that child is being intensely rejecting of this connection seems to me to be a Herculean challenge.

It is difficult to stay curious when a child continually responds with challenge and disconnection. Empathy is easily lost in the face of this onslaught. Perhaps the hardest part of the attitude to maintain, however, is acceptance. Accepting the thoughts, feelings, beliefs, wishes and desires of the child without evaluation, resisting the temptation to try and change this experience through reassurance, 'telling' the child to feel differently. When the child's emotional experience is distressing or difficult it is understandable that the parent moves to evaluation – this is not a good way to feel; you need to feel differently. The parent wants the child's experience to be different, to be more comfortable for both of them, and so she attempts to change the child's experience. Security comes, however, from the parent accepting the child's experience and sitting with this, however uncomfortable.

This next story was written for these parents. I, too, have had to learn acceptance, to sit with them in their discomfort and distress, not able to change their emotional experience. I can't persuade them that they are good parents, doing a good job, if they are feeling a profound sense of failure, of not being good enough. I can, however, understand their experience and empathize with them. I have found that my acceptance of their experience helps them to stay with it, accepting their child's distress and managing to maintain PACE even in the face of extremely challenging and rejecting behaviours. My PACE for them does help them to experience themselves in subtle but different ways, and this in turn helps them to have a deeper acceptance for themselves and their children. This story is about acceptance and the profound impact it can have on all of us.

Longing and Belonging

There was once a young maiden, lonely and afraid in the world. Her life had been hard and she thought little of herself. She moved around a lot, sometimes staying with this group of people for a while and sometimes with another, but never did she stay for long. One day this young maiden had a baby, a bonny child, who looked up into her eyes asking to be taken care of. But this young maiden thought little of herself; how could she think about a baby? I am sad to say, the baby's needs were neglected, and soon she stopped looking into her mother's eyes.

Now there happened to be in the same town a beautiful lady; her hair was blonde and reached down to her waist, and her eyes were blue and twinkled with kindness. This lady loved most of all to make other people happy. She had one great sadness in her life, however – she had no child of her own. She wished for a child to love and cherish, a child who could be happy in her care. Her husband was sad for her; he saw his wife making others happy, and he longed to give her this one thing, but it was not to be.

One day, as they were both out walking, the lady and the maiden happened to meet. The lady felt sad to see the young lady, so alone and afraid.

"How can I help you?" she said.

"I think little of myself," said the maiden, "you cannot help me. Maybe one day I will find happiness, but it will not be from you."

The lady was greatly saddened by this. "Please let me take care of you. I wish only for your happiness."

But the maiden was not to be moved in this. "No, I have to wander in the world for some time yet. You cannot make me happy; but there is one thing you can do for me. Take this baby of mine. I think little of myself, how can I think of her? Help this baby to grow big and strong; I hope she can be happy in your care."

The lady was overjoyed. It was as if she had met her fairy godmother and all her dreams had been granted. She gladly took the child from the maiden.

"Come too," she said, "I will help you both to be happy." But no, the maiden had already turned away.

So the lady and her husband left this town and found a place to live that had all a young child needed. They called the baby Felicity, as they wished only for her happiness. If happiness could come from having what you need, then Felicity would have been happy indeed. She had a mother and father who cared greatly for her, she had a bedroom fit for a princess, she had all the clothes she could want, she had toys, she had food, she had warmth. Sometimes they said no to her, and of course they made sure she went to school – having all that you need is not always having all that you want! But most of all, Felicity had parents who looked into her eyes and who thought about her.

Having what you need is part of being happy, but being able to use what you have is also important. Felicity was comfortable in the house, with her bedroom and her toys. She was warm and well fed, but when her parents looked into her eyes, Felicity did not look back. She had looked into her first mother's eyes and it was frightening to her; she did not risk it again. She grew big and strong. She grew even bonnier in face and healthy in body, but always there was a great longing within her. She could not be happy. She longed for her first mother to think about her. She longed to be able to look and see her first mother looking back.

Deep inside Felicity, anger started to grow. She longed for her first mother, and she began to believe that this first mother was all that she needed. She even forgot that she had looked into the eyes of her first mother and her mother had not looked back. She began to believe that only with her could she be happy – her first mother would give her what she wanted, her first mother would never say no to her or make her go to school when she did not want to. Her anger and distress grew as she came to believe that her mother prevented this. Her mother had taken her away from her first mother; if it wasn't for this mother, she would be with her first mother now. She turned her anger towards her mother. She resisted her embraces; she would not take her food; she could not enjoy being with her. She shouted at her to go away and leave her alone.

And as Felicity's anger grew, she became more and more alone. A great river developed around her which flowed faster and faster as her distress grew stronger. Felicity sat on a small raft and was swept along the river. Her mother feared for Felicity. She was so sad that she had not been able to make Felicity happy, but she did not give up on her. "Look at me," she said. "I will help you." But Felicity was angry with her mother, and was afraid to look. She clung to her raft and looked ahead as the turbulent water swept her along.

But her mother still did not give up; she ran along the shore calling to Felicity. "I will help you," she said. "I will not give up on you." She kept pace with the raft and thought about how to rescue Felicity from the river that was threatening to sweep her away.

First, she still tried to take care of her. She ensured she had food and blankets to keep Felicity warm. "Take these," she said. "They will protect you." But Felicity did not reach out, and the food and blankets were swept away.

Next, she told Felicity of all the things she would do for her as her mother. She told her that mothers wanted their children to be happy. She would get her what she wanted, she would cuddle her when she needed this, but mothers also kept their children safe. Sometimes she would say no to her. Sometimes she would ensure that she did things even if she didn't want to because she knew only then could Felicity be happy. Felicity heard the words but did not believe them. "You stole me," she said. "You do not want me to be happy."

The raft slowed and the mother saw a small chance. "Come to me," called her mother. "Leave the raft and hold on to me. I will keep you safe." She stood there, arms out, but Felicity did not dare to look, she did not dare to reach out to her. Instead her anger became bigger. She shouted words of hatred and the raft took off again.

As her anger grew, the river flowed faster, but still the mother kept pace with the little raft. She thought hard and wondered if Felicity needed to hear the story of her birth again. Maybe then she could believe in the strength of her mother's arms and the power of her love. She told Felicity of the young maiden who was lonely and afraid, of how she could not think about herself, never mind a tiny baby. She described how the maiden found her and asked her to care for her baby. She did not seek her own happiness, only her child's. Felicity heard the words, but she could not believe them. "No," she shouted. "This cannot be. You took me from her. You have not given me happiness, only longing is in my heart."

And the river flowed faster.

And the mother despaired.

The mother almost stopped running to keep up with the raft. She almost let her child go, but she was strong. She kept on going although her heart was breaking, and this strength gave her wisdom. Wisdom whispered in her ear: don't give up. You can still reach her, but you will need to go to her. Stop trying to rescue her from the raft; accept that she is angry and frightened and confused; join her instead. Sit with her in her distress.

And then the mother knew what to do. She swam out into the river and climbed onto the raft.

"Go away," said Felicity. "I do not want you here."

"I will not leave you," said her mother. "You need me. I will stay with you. I will accept your anger, and your longing. I will not leave you. I am your mother and this is what mothers do. I wanted your happiness, but I will stay with you in your sadness and your longing and your despair."

At first Felicity resisted. She did not believe her mother. She did not want her help, but her mother remained. Her strength and her acceptance made both of them strong; slowly, oh so slowly, the river slowed.

"I cannot look at you," said Felicity. "I'm afraid of what I will see."

"I know," said her mother. "I will keep looking at you until you are ready."

"I'm afraid," said Felicity, "that your care will take me further away from what I long for. I do not want your food and your blankets."

"I know," said her mother. "My looking after you is scary."

"I hate you when you say 'no' to me," said Felicity. "If you won't let me do what I want, I think you do not love me."

"I know," said her mother. "I cannot give you everything you want, but I will give you everything you need. That is how you will know that I love you."

"I long for my first mother," said Felicity. "You took me away from her. You are the cause of my unhappiness. If I were with her still, all would be well."

"I know," said her mother. "It feels like I stole you from her. I want you to understand your first mother's story, but it is too scary for you right now. I will stay with you until you are ready to hear it. I want you to be happy, but I will stay with you even though you are sad and lonely and scared."

And finally, finally, Felicity could tell her mother the biggest fear of all.

A fear so big that she had hidden from it all her life.

A fear so terrible that she worried thinking about it might make it true.

A fear so dangerous that she thought it would lead to her losing everything.

"I am afraid," said Felicity. "I am afraid that I am bad. That is why my first mother gave me away. That is why you will leave me. I will be all alone. I daren't look at you for fear I will see it is true."

And then her mother cried, for she felt so sad for Felicity. "What a big and horrible fear. I cannot make the fear go away. I have been trying to do that all your life and all it has led to is this raft on this river. But I will stay with you. I will hold you and I will help you to carry the fear."

And as she held on to Felicity, the river slowed and became smaller. The raft grew bigger, and gradually, gradually, it drifted to the shore.

Do not imagine that this happened all at once. A big fear takes a long time to go; but slowly, slowly, mother and daughter together found the way. One day the raft was big enough and strong enough to take them to the shore. They got out and found father there, waiting for them. He embraced them and they all set off for home. Felicity looked up into the eyes of her mother and father and finally she could see the love and care that she had longed for all along.

They lived together happily ever after.

Except, of course, that such an outcome would make this a fairy story; in truth, they had many ups and downs together. Sometimes the fear grew big again and Felicity found herself back on the raft. Sometimes her mother stayed on the shore, experiencing the despair that comes with watching progress going backwards. But always Wisdom stayed with her, and drawing strength from Wisdom meant that the mother could stay with Felicity whilst the fear subsided again. Felicity learned that she was not bad, but that life was full of many turns. She had a family she belonged to and this, in the end, was enough. Felicity found that what she really longed for was right there, waiting for her.

Notes about Part VI

Stories, whether written for children or adults, can be helpful for parents. A story can convey the experience of a child in ways that simply describing this experience cannot. Parents and other adults in the children's lives can gain an increased understanding of the children and their struggles through the simple narratives. Academic books have their place, but stories can be much more powerful. Stories have a unique way of conveying theory and understanding. The narratives can therefore facilitate understanding about child development and the impact of abuse, neglect and separation on a child's development, behaviour and capacity to trust.

Therapeutic stories written for children are therefore also for the adults caring for them. Once I was reading a story to a young boy as he sat with his father. As I finished, this father said to me that he felt the story was not only for his son but also for him. He recognized that this story was giving him an insight into the experience of his child which would be helpful to him in his attempts to respond with PACE and emotional connection.

All the stories in this book are therefore created for adults as well as for children. By sharing them with the children, and witnessing their response to these stories, the adults understand the children at a different level.

In addition, creating stories directly for the parents can be another way of collaboratively working together to help explore, understand and support the children. These stories can be created for, created together or created by the parent. Each will be a starting point for some additional shared experience of the child and of the parents' response to the child.

For example, a parent responded to the story of 'William and Edward' with a feeling of despair and hopelessness, and complained bitterly to me that I had written a story about a super-mother, holding up an ideal that she could not live up to. She could not see herself ever being able to respond as empathically as the mother did within the story. This opened the door for us to explore this parent's fears and doubts. We discovered together that the lack of empathy she had experienced during her childhood was linked to her current discomfort in providing empathy for her children. She always had a lingering fear that she was somehow giving in, or letting them get away with things. Following this exploration of her experience we were able to return to a focus on parenting strategies with this deeper understanding.

Parents can respond to these stories in a variety of ways. Sometimes they immediately like them and are able to resonate with the experience that has been explored. At other times they may need some time to reflect on the story, absorbing its meaning slowly as they read it to themselves. Parents can be inspired to create and share their own stories with their children or to sit with their children and create stories together.

Responses are not always positive, however. Sometimes the parents are angry. The narrative can trigger shame or anxiety that they are not being good enough in their parenting of their child, that they are letting him down in some way. If he had a different parent, more like the parent in the story, the child might be doing better. They might even view the narrative as criticism or disappointment from the practitioner who chose the story. Such responses are really important and should not be dismissed or responded to defensively. If the practitioner can stay open and engaged with the parent, these very honest responses can be the starting point for some helpful exploration of the parent's own emotional experience. Shared understanding of this and a chance for the parent to feel deeply accepted by the practitioner can lead to increased resilience and a stronger capacity to parent the child.

The stories in this part therefore illustrate some of the ways that stories can be created for parents. Whether biographical or metaphorical, these narratives can provide a useful addition to collaborative working with parents.

Part VII
STORIES FOR PRACTITIONERS

Story 19

The Finest Forest in all the Land

Story type: Insight

Themes: Multi-agency working; Working in partnership; Health, Education and Social Work

Age range: Adults

Children and young people who have experienced abuse, neglect, separation and loss are highly vulnerable, with a complex range of needs. Some have had such difficult experiences that decisions have been made to remove them from their birth families, a drastic intervention that adds trauma on top of trauma. Whilst Children's Services work hard to provide these children with loving and stable families, professional support cannot end here. All families caring for highly traumatized children deserve understanding and sensitive, long-term support from all agencies. In addition, if children and their families are to recover from the trauma they have experienced, professionals from across agencies will need to work closely together.

Multi-agency working allows professionals to provide supportive interventions that will meet the complex and broad needs of this vulnerable group of children and their families. Multi-agency working facilitates good working together across agencies and disciplines. This close working together is at the heart of interventions that will promote mental health and emotional wellbeing for all family members.

Working together allows good sharing of information, but more importantly, these open channels of communication lead to a shared understanding of the support and therapy needs of the families and family members. Through close working together, practitioners gain a greater understanding of the roles of other practitioners. This ensures referrals between services are made in a timely and appropriate manner. It also reduces conflicting advice and inappropriate demands being made on families. These families benefit when all agencies work closely together.

This story was written for a colleague of mine. Wendy embraced multi-agency working and kept this central to all her practice. Services benefited from her focus and commitment to this ideal, and in turn, the children and families at the centre of these services experienced a higher level of sensitive, timely and needed support. I wrote this story as a way of honouring the expertise she brought to multi-agency working.

The Finest Forest in all the Land

A great forest grows from saplings, young and tender; saplings that need caring for, protecting and educating if they are to grow to maturity.

This was the task of the three forest spirits:

- Nadiyya, the tender one, cared for and nurtured the saplings.

- Tenzin, the educator, ensured the saplings had the knowledge they needed to grow tall and strong.

- Shamira, the protector, kept the saplings safe – secure from the dangers that might threaten them.

Each spirit worked hard, passionate in their task. They wanted to see the saplings grow to maturity, to help a great forest emerge from the potential that these youngsters represented. No one could doubt their commitment, yet despite their dedication, there was a problem. The saplings were not thriving. They grew slowly; they lacked the vigour to make a great forest. The spirits were troubled; they could see that they were failing, and this distressed them greatly.

Nadiyya redoubled her efforts to take care of the saplings. She ensured that they had the correct amount of sunlight and water. She checked that the soil was full of the nutrients they needed. Only if they were healthy would the trees thrive. Hers was the most important task. If she could give them health, then surely the forest would be the finest of all.

Tenzin searched amongst his great library for wisdom to guide him. He wanted to ensure that his teaching was the best it could be. If he could give the trees the knowledge they needed, then surely they would grow tall and strong. His was the most important task. The trees needed learning; only then would the forest be the finest of all.

Shamira remained vigilant for any sign of danger. She protected the trees from pests and stormy weather – anything that might harm them. Only if they were kept safe would they be able to grow to be majestic in their maturity. Hers was the most important task. The trees needed safety so that the forest could be the finest of all.

And so the three spirits worked tirelessly. Yet their endeavours were not bearing fruit. Still the saplings grew slowly and weak.

Suniti was a spirit guide sent to help the three forest spirits, and she was troubled. She could see how hard the forest spirits were working, but she could also see how much they were struggling. She needed to find a way to help them.

Suniti went to each in turn.

Nadiyya was glad of Suniti's interest. "You see how important it is to care for the saplings. Please aid me with my task. I need help to gather more nutrients; I need more time to take care of them. Give me these things and I am sure the forest will thrive."

Tenzin welcomed Suniti. "Ah, at last you see how important my teachings are. Give me more wisdom and time to let me impart this extra wisdom to the trees. If I have more time and learning I know the forest will grow tall and strong."

Shamira also invited Suniti to help her. "They need more protection," she said. "There are dangers everywhere. Let me have help to seek out the threats. If I can have the time to keep the saplings safe, then I know the forest will grow to be as strong and majestic as we all hope."

Suniti listened to these requests and knew they were not unreasonable. She wished to help each of them. She could see that each wanted the same thing. The three spirits were all working for the greater good of the forest. Each was looking after the saplings in the way they knew best.

Yet Suniti remained troubled. She did not think more time, more learning or more help would make the difference that the spirits thought they would. There needed to be another way.

And so Suniti approached the three spirits. "Come with me," she said. "Let us spend some time together and seek the answers that we all want. Together we will find a way of bringing these saplings to maturity, the finest forest we can imagine."

The spirits, who were all good in their hearts, saw the wisdom in this, and so they willingly followed Suniti. Together they took the time to consider what they should do. At first this was hard. Each continued to argue for their own needs, certain that their answer was the way forward.

Nadiyya spoke to the others. "Yes, the saplings need protecting, and of course they need teaching; but they must be healthy. Let me make them strong and then your protection and teaching will be of some use."

Tenzin argued: "No, learning comes first. When these saplings know what they must do, they will grow. Yes, they need protecting and health, but what good will these be if they are not taught how to grow strong and tall?"

And of course Shamira remained convinced of the importance of protection: "Your learning and your health can wait. Let me protect them; only when they are truly safe will they be able to devote their resources to health and growth."

Suniti watched and listened. She asked each of them questions. She acknowledged their commitment and their skill. Each of them grew in confidence and hope as she listened without judging, as she questioned and reflected with them. She drew from each of them their passion and their knowledge and ensured that each learned this from the others.

Nadiyya talked about how to help each sapling gain the health needed. She spoke with intelligence and in depth, confident that Suniti was listening to her. And she noticed Tenzin and Shamira listening too. They all came to a greater understanding of the health needs of the saplings.

Tenzin, too, found his knowledge was respected. As he spoke, wisely sharing all his lore, he became even more articulate under Suniti's kind gaze. They all benefited from his insightful teachings and knew a little better how to help the saplings gain the wisdom they needed to ensure that they reached their very best potential.

And Shamira talked urgently about the need for protection. She was not dismissed either. Of course the saplings needed to be kept safe. How could they grow if there were dangers encroaching upon them? Suniti helped Shamira to share her profound understanding about how to keep the saplings safe, and they all grew in skill about how to safeguard the young trees.

As they all talked with passion, knowledge and commitment, Suniti helped them to share this understanding.

And so the knowledge and understanding of the forest spirits was combined. They each learned from the others and the total was far, far greater than the parts.

Nadiyya, Tenzin and Shamira now understood that each of their skills was important. Only when the saplings were healthy, safe and wise would they grow into the forest of their dreams. The forest spirits did not need more time, more help or more understanding. They had all they needed, and by combining their knowledge, the forest would grow strong, healthy and with the majesty of all their dreams.

The young saplings were indeed well looked after. Now they started to grow tall and straight. Suniti had ensured that the three spirits continued to use their individual skills to give the saplings what they needed, but the three were now one in helping the forest to grow in strength and health and majesty.

The forest did indeed become the finest forest in all the land.

Story 20

Never You Mind

Story type: Solution

Themes: Therapist's experience of resistance; Providing therapy; Acceptance; Curiosity; Empathy

Age range: Adults

In a former publication I wrote about using therapy with children living in foster and adoptive homes. I reflected on Sarah:

> Sarah, a pale, thin 14-year-old girl, sits in front of me. She has to leave her five-year foster placement. The carers cannot cope with the constant lying, stealing and fighting. Sarah cannot cope with the false promises from her mum that she will be able to return. She sits in front of me now and pours out her anger at a friend who has recently let her down. I hear the anger Sarah feels at a placement breaking down, at a mother who cannot be there for her but most of all at herself for not being good enough. I sit there and listen and wonder how can I help? What intervention can help Sarah through a childhood that has let her down? What psychological theory can help me to understand the fear and dread of matching yourself to the world and finding yourself lacking? I struggle to find a way to help. I fear for Sarah's future. (Golding 2006, p.305)

In this next story I reflect upon what I have learned about therapy since I worked with Sarah. The motivations, the despair and the fear of not being able to 'fix' the children referred to us is the backdrop of my journey in working therapeutically with developmentally traumatized children.

Acceptance by the therapist can also be difficult, as it is for the parents. We witness the children's pain and trauma and we want to make a difference. In our minds, making a difference can become synonymous with 'fixing' the children, making the distress go away. We are under pressure from others too. Therapy is seen as an answer, but maybe not so much an answer for the children but an answer to our own discomfort as we observe the children's distress. The child is in pain; we want the pain to go away. The child is misbehaving; we want the child to behave better. The child is dependent; we want the child to become independent.

We may not be able to fix the children but we can help them. Sitting with the uncomfortable, sharing their stories and making sense of their experience is all part of the journey we go on with the child.

> Moving children into foster and adoptive homes provides an improved environment and the opportunity for better relationships. It is anticipated that the children will then change their behaviour. The behaviour that has been successful in their early lives is unsuccessful in their new life and causes them problems. It is hoped that they will adapt, developing loving relationships within their family, a positive approach to learning in school and successful friendships within the community. Often however this doesn't happen. A common response to this is to suggest that the child has a problem. Therapy is seen as a way of fixing this problem. The child is not benefiting from the love and protection now being provided, and therefore needs some 'expert' help. This is the myth of 'fixing the child'. The desire to have the child fit in to a new world. (Golding 2006, p.322)

I have learned that to truly help a child we need to join her in her world; when we do this, we offer her a relationship that can truly lead to transformation in all of us. The goal isn't the point, however; the journey is.

Never You Mind

Jack was a fine youth, big and strong. He was kind and cheerful, with a caring heart and a friendly smile. He had good people caring for him, and friends to pass his time with. To see him like this no one would know the trouble he had experienced earlier in life. This was something he did not talk about; he preferred people to know him as he was now, not to view him through the lens of his past.

"Never you mind" he would say. "It's no good dwelling on things you can't change."

But the past can mark you out despite yourself, and trouble ignored can build into a burden that goes with you throughout your life. Jack carried an affliction with him. He was burdened by a large hump on his back, a hump that was growing bigger with each passing year. Jack now walked with a stoop because of the weight of this hump. Not that it seemed to bother him; he just continued as if nothing was there. Everyone could see it, but Jack appeared oblivious as he calmly got on with his life. If anyone mentioned it, Jack just looked at them with a puzzled look. "What hump?" They tried to tell him what they could see, but Jack just laughed.

"Never you mind," he would say. "It's no good dwelling on things you can't see."

And so it continued. Jack got on with his life; at 16 he left school and was apprenticed as a carpenter. He even thought about building his own house one day. He looked to the future whilst his past continued to burden him, unnoticed.

This was a situation that did not go unnoticed by the community's wise woman, Shona. She knew Jack and worried about him. She hoped she might help him. She understood the nature of his affliction and believed she could make it go away. She offered to help Jack. He was very courteous to her. He allowed her to meet him and to talk to him. He was happy to share stories with her, but always these stories stayed in the present. He would never talk about his past. He was not rude, but he quietly ignored her attempts to go there, or he would distract her with anecdotes from the present. If she mentioned this to him, he simply smiled.

"Never you mind," he would say. "It's no good dwelling on things long gone."

Shona tried to help Jack, but whatever way she came at it, he quietly resisted her. She tried to talk about it slowly and gently; she tried a direct approach. Sometimes she talked in stories or metaphors. She talked indirectly, drawing on the experience of other people she had known; she talked directly. Whatever she did, nothing seemed to help. Jack would smile, and quietly deflect her. He would talk animatedly about carpentry, fondly about friends, with tenderness about the parents who took care of him, but never would he look back to the past. The hump remained. Shona tried talking about the burden he carried and her belief that she could help him get rid of it. He looked quizzically at her: "What burden?" he asked. "Never you mind," he would say. "It's no good dwelling on things you don't notice."

Shona felt frustrated. She wanted so much to make things better for Jack. She truly believed she knew how to help him, how to get rid of the hump once and for all. She feared for him if he kept ignoring it. If the hump continued growing, she did not know what would happen to him in the future, but Jack wouldn't let her help. She was running out of ideas.

Shona turned to a dear friend of hers. He had been her mentor for many a year, and she appreciated his wisdom, which was greater than hers. She poured out her frustration and her anguish that she did not appear to be helping Jack, despite all her efforts. Jack's burden was becoming hers and she did not know what to do next. Her mentor asked a few questions and commented on how hard she had been working and how much she wanted to help Jack. He sympathized with her frustration, and expressed empathy for her sadness that nothing she did appeared to be making a difference. Shona felt herself lightening as he talked with her. The burden of how to help Jack seemed less as she reflected on his words. Suddenly Shona smiled; her friend's kind words did not tell her what to do, no words of advice, but wisdom nonetheless. Sometimes a burden is a burden, and by joining her in hers, he had shown her what she needed to do.

Shona returned to Jack. She was curious about how he managed – how he kept on smiling, how he kept on dreaming. She commented on how hard things could be still, how hard he had to work for the things that other people had without effort. Jack told her of his satisfaction in what he had, and acknowledged that sometimes he did feel sad, even despairing at times. He kept on smiling because that is all he knew to do when things seemed hard. Shona shared his joy in what he had achieved, but also expressed her sadness that Jack had come to this through difficulty and hardship.

"Never you mind," Jack said. "It's no good dwelling on things that are, but I am glad you are with me."

As Jack walked away he seemed more erect and less weighed down by the hump. Shona smiled; sometimes you can't get rid of a burden, but you can share it and it gets less in the process. She had less fear for Jack now. His past would always be there, his burden would not go away, but lighter now his future beckoned, and Shona had hope in her heart.

Story 21

Bridge Over Troubled Water

Story type: Insight

Themes: Providing services; The helping relationship

Age range: Adults

I offer this final story as a reflection about practitioners who choose to work with troubled children, young people and their families. This is a story for practitioners and the commissioners who have responsibility for providing the services.

The relationships practitioners offer can provide understanding, support, inspiration, hope and healing. This takes time, however. Children who have experienced trauma, abuse and neglect in their early lives often struggle emotionally. Children living in foster care, adoptive homes or in other substitute families have the additional trauma of loss and separation. All these children are less likely to be helped by short-term interventions and quick fixes. They need practitioners who are enabled to take the time to truly understand, and who can support the families alongside the children. The children and young people cannot 'recover' from their early experience, but they can learn to live with their experience and become more resilient in the process. Short-term fixes hold out the false promise of recovery; long-term interventions provide the support that is needed if resilience is to be truly developed.

When we meet families, they are already on a journey. It is a privilege to go on part of that journey with them, and to make the journey a little easier in the process.

With thanks to Paul Simon and Art Garfunkel for their inspirational song, and for the title that I have borrowed for this final story.

Bridge Over Troubled Water

Far away from here there is a village. It is just an ordinary village, with people going about their ordinary business. As is the way with some villages, this is a village that many people pass through on the journeys they are taking.

Running through this village is a river. This is no ordinary river. It is full of the most turbulent and fast-running water that you will ever see. Anyone passing through the village must cross this river in order to continue with their journey.

The villagers are a kindly people. They can see the struggles people have trying to cross the river so that they can continue with their journeys. They wish to help. And so they appoint someone to act as a guide for crossing the river. The guide knows the best way to cross and can offer good advice which, if taken, provides people with a bridge to make the crossing easier. This is because the guide is initiated into the secrets of the river. For long ago there was a bridge that helped people cross, but an enchantment was put on this bridge. There may have been a good reason for the enchantment at the time, but that reason is now lost to memory. Only the knowledge of the bridge remains. To find it, the person must enter the river at the most turbulent spot of all. They must step in confidently without looking back. Only then will they find their feet on the bridge that will help them to safely cross.

Time and time again the guide offers advice to the people wanting to cross. He shows the exact spot they need to enter the river, and gives precise instructions about how to do this. Time and time again this good advice is not followed. The person looks at the river and sees the fast-running water. It does not make sense to enter where it is most turbulent; just a few spaces down it appears calmer. Some people choose to enter where it looks calmer. Others enter where shown, but look back, fearful of making the next step. Some people stand on the bank, watching, but fearing to enter.

The guide can only watch as these people struggle. They get swept down river by the hidden currents that are strongest where it appears calmest. They get caught up in the jetsam and flotsam that has caught up at the edge of the bank at this turbulent spot. They become stuck on the bank unable to go on with their journey. The villagers are saddened that they cannot be more helpful to these people.

Now one day there arrived in the village an older person. This was a wise man or perhaps a woman – it is hard to say, as he or she was dressed in a long cape and a hood. The guide stepped forward to meet this visitor. He enquired if he could help in the crossing of the river. The wise person told him no, he was there to help him cross.

"But I don't need to cross the river," protested the guide. "My job is to help others to cross."

"Ah," said the wise person. "That is your problem. If you want to help people to safely cross the river then you need to enter it yourself. Only if you go in with them will they find the bridge and thus safely cross over."

"But that will take longer," protested the guide. "Surely if they follow my advice they can get across more quickly and I am ready for the next visitor?"

"But that is not working, is it?" pointed out the wise person. "The visitors are taking longer to struggle across the river, and many never get across at all. Some of them end up back on this bank and they have to come back to you for more advice. Others are just stuck in the village, never finding a way to cross. Do as I say, and you will help many more people to get across."

This was a revelation to the guide, and to all the villagers. Never had they thought to enter the river with the visitors. Sure enough this was the answer they needed. By entering the river as well, they could help the visitor to find the bridge and thus to safely cross the river. It did take longer, and with some inconvenience, but from that day on, many more visitors were able to find the bridge and safely cross the troubled water.

Notes about Part VII

I wanted to include some stories for practitioners within this book in recognition that we are all in this together — child, parent and practitioner. In essence, of course, all of these stories are written for all of us. My hope is that they can increase insight, helping us to share a deeper understanding of the insecure and emotionally troubled child. My expertise has developed in working with children living in substitute homes — adopted, fostered or residential — or living in other alternative families. Many of the stories therefore reflect my experience with these children and their families, although I hope they also provide support for those caring for and helping children wherever they are living.

These final stories have given me an opportunity to move outwards from the child and family to the wider service structures and the support that we offer to these families. The services we provide within Health, Education and Social Care are an important reflection of how we cherish those who are vulnerable within our communities and our society at large. Perhaps stories can help us to keep the children and families at the centre of this provision, however restricted we are by budgets, resources and timescales.

APPENDICES

Appendix 1
PLANNING A SOLUTION STORY

Theme, emotional problem experienced	
What do you want your story to be about? Who are you creating the story for? (the 'reader') Are you mirroring a situation? How direct or metaphorical do you want to be?	
The setting	
Where is the story taking place? Settings can be fantastical, as in fairy stories or fantasies; futuristic, as in science fiction; or a modern-day setting.	
Main character or characters (hero or protagonist)	
Who is going to be the central character? This can be a person, animal, object or plant/tree. Choose a character that will resonate with the 'reader'. The character will have the adventure, go on a journey or try to solve a problem.	
Theme, problem or challenge faced	
This might be a difficulty, task, threat or danger that faces the main character or the community where the main character lives. Are there any obstacles that stand in the way?	

Helpers	
Who assists the main character in his or her journey and helps to solve the problem? Often characters have some extra wisdom that the main character can use to find that he has the solution within himself.	
Are there any objects of special significance?	
There might be things in the story that have special significance or magical properties. A symbol might be used to show the process of change, to represent hope or the power of assistance and support from others.	
The resolution	
How the problem is overcome. This is the conclusion or ending to the story. It is usually a happy ending, although it does not have to be.	
Prizes gained	
This is the result for the main character or his community. Often the 'message' of the story is linked to the prize gained.	

Appendix 2[1]
PLANNING A THERAPEUTIC STORY

Theme, emotional problem experienced Identify the emotional problem or issue that the story will be about.	
The setting This setting provides a metaphorical context for the problem or issue. The setting describes the place and the situation.	
Main character or characters (hero or protagonist) The main characters will represent the person or people who are struggling with the emotional problem.	
How will the character encounter the problem? How will the character encounter the metaphorical problem? How will the struggle be represented? Include a representation of unhelpful coping strategies that are being used in real life. How does the story indicate that these are unhelpful? How will this lead to a crisis which will lead to a change in coping strategy?	

---

1   See Sunderland (2000).

Crisis to solution	
How will the story represent the shift from crisis to solution? Who or what might appear to help the main character move towards a solution? How will the solution be represented? For example, in the form of a new coping strategy or a more creative way of dealing with this situation?	
The resolution	
What new behaviour or attitude will the main character display as he changes direction? This might be a new behaviour, new way of being or different way of coping. How will this alter his experience of himself, others or the world?	

Appendix 3
PLANNING A TRAUMA STORY

Theme, trauma experienced	
What traumatic experience do you want to represent in the story?	
The setting	
Where is the story taking place?	
Main character or characters (hero or protagonist)	
How will you represent the person who has experienced the trauma? How will you represent this character experiencing the trauma? Are there other characters in the story?	
Making sense	
How will the character in the story make sense of the trauma as it is being experienced within the narrative? This will represent the processing of the trauma.	
Helpers	
Who will assist the main character to make sense of the trauma? This will represent the integration of the traumatic experience.	

The resolution	
How would you like to end the story? This ending will represent the hope that the trauma is survivable and the individual can get on with his or her life.	

Appendix 4
PLANNING A NARRATIVE TO EXPLORE LIFE STORY

Theme, life experience being explored What life experience would you like to explore in the story? Think about the experience of the child, and also the family characteristics that you would like to mirror, including parents, siblings and other significant people in the child's life.	
The setting What setting would you like to use to mirror the child's own setting, where she experienced the life you are exploring?	
Main character or characters (hero or protagonist) What characters will you use to represent the child and other family or significant individuals in the child's life?	
Fear and hope How will you represent the fears or worries that the life experience has left the child with? How will you build hope into the story that things can be different?	

Helpers	
Who will you introduce into the story to help the child overcome the fears and worries and believe in the hope?	
The resolution	
How will you conclude the story? This ending will often mirror the experience you would like the child to find with her current or future family.	

Appendix 5
PLANNING AN INSIGHT STORY

Theme, insight being offered	
What do you want your story to be about? Think about the understanding that you would like this story to convey. This will be the theme of the story.	
The setting	
Where is the story taking place? Think about a scenario that will help to portray the situation or attitude that you would like to illustrate.	
Main character or characters (hero or protagonist)	
Who are going to be the characters in the story? These characters will be used to explore the theme of the story.	
The problem	
What will be the problem, dilemma or issue that the characters will face? This will help you to convey the theme of the story. It might illustrate a stuckness because of a maladaptive coping strategy being used by the main character.	

Helpers	
Who assists the main character in solving the problem, thus illustrating the new understanding which can help move things forward?	
The resolution	
How is the problem overcome? This is the conclusion or ending to the story. It represents the new understanding and how, with this, the situation can be improved.	

References

Bettelheim, B. (1991) *The Uses of Enchantment. The Meaning and Importance of Fairy Tales.* London: Penguin Books Ltd. (First published by Thames & Hudson, 1976.)

Cattanach, A. (2008) 'Working Creatively with Children and Their Families After Trauma. The Storied Life.' In C.A. Malchiodi (ed.) *Creative Interventions with Traumatized Children* (Chapter 10). New York: The Guilford Press.

Dutton, D. (2010) *The Art Instinct. Beauty, Pleasure and Human Evolution.* Oxford: Oxford University Press.

Freeman, J., Epston, D. and Lobovits, D. (1997) *Playful Approaches to Serious Problems. Narrative Therapy with Children and Their Families.* New York: W.W. Norton & Co. Inc.

Golding, K.S. (2006) 'Opening the Door. How Can Therapy Help the Child and Young Person Living in Foster or Adoptive Homes?' In K.S. Golding, H.R. Dent, R. Nissim and E. Stott (eds) *Thinking Psychologically about Children Who Are Looked After and Adopted. Space for Reflection* (Chapter 11). Hoboken, NJ: John Wiley & Sons Ltd.

Golding, K.S. (2008) *Nurturing Attachments. Supporting Children Who Are Fostered or Adopted.* London: Jessica Kingsley Publishers.

Golding, K.S. (2014) *Nurturing Attachments Training Resource. Running Parenting Groups for Adoptive Parents and Foster or Kinship Carers.* London: Jessica Kingsley Publishers.

Golding, K.S. and Hughes, D.A. (2012) *Creating Loving Attachments. Parenting with PACE to Nurture Confidence and Security in the Troubled Child.* London: Jessica Kingsley Publishers.

Grosz, S. (2013) *The Examined Life. How We Lose and Find Ourselves.* London: Chatto & Windus.

Hughes, D.A. (2009) *Attachment Focused Parenting. Effective Strategies to Care for Children.* New York: W.W. Norton & Co. Inc.

Hughes, D.A. (2011) *Attachment Focused Family Therapy. The Workbook.* New York: W.W. Norton & Co. Inc.

Hughes, D.A. and Baylin, J. (2012) *Brain-Based Parenting. The Neuroscience of Caregiving for Healthy Attachment.* New York: W.W. Norton & Co. Inc.

Ironside, V. (1996) *The Huge Bag of Worries.* London: Macdonald Young Books.

Jennings, S. (2004) *Creative Storytelling with Children at Risk.* Milton Keynes: Speechmark Publishing Ltd.

Killick, S. and Boffey, M. (2012) *Building Relationships through Storytelling. A Foster Carer's Guide to Attachment and Stories.* London: The Fostering Network.

Lacher, D.B., Nichols, T. and May, J.C. (2005) *Connecting with Kids through Stories*. London: Jessica Kingsley Publishers.

Malchiodi, C.A. and Ginns-Gruenberg, D. (2008) 'Trauma, Loss and Bibliotherapy. The Healing Power of Stories.' In C.A. Malchiodi (ed.) *Creative Interventions with Traumatized Children* (Chapter 8). New York: The Guilford Press.

Moore, J. (2012) *Once Upon a Time. Stories and Drama to Use in Direct Work with Adopted and Fostered Children*. London: BAAF.

Parkinson, R. (2009) *Transforming Tales. How Stories Can Change People*. London: Jessica Kingsley Publishers.

Salans, M. (2009) *Storytelling with Children in Crisis. Take Just One Step – How Impoverished Children Heal through Stories*. London: Jessica Kingsley Publishers.

Steinbeck, J. (1930) 'In Awe of Words.' *The Exonian*. Exeter University.

Sunderland, M. (2000) *Using Story Telling as a Therapeutic Tool with Children*. Milton Keynes: Speechmark Publishing Ltd.

Sunderland, M. (2001) *Using Storytelling as a Therapeutic Tool with Children*. Milton Keynes: Speechmark Publishing Ltd.

Thomas, T. and Killick, S. (2007) *Telling Tales. Storytelling as Emotional Literacy*. Blackburn: Educational Printing Services Ltd.

Vetere, A. and Dowling, E. (eds) (2005) *Narrative Therapies with Children and Their Families. A Practitioner's Guide to Concepts and Approach*. Hove: Routledge.

White, M. (2004) *Narrative Practice and Exotic Lives. Resurrecting Diversity in Everyday Life*. Adelaide, Australia: Dulwich Centre Publications.

White, M. and Epston, D. (1990) *Narrative Means to Therapeutic Ends*. London: W.W. Norton & Co Inc.

Index